Dear Tom

The Rosary is your strength.

Pray often.

[signature]

The Rosary

The Life of Jesus and Mary

Bob and Penny Lord

Journeys of Faith
1-800-633-2484

Other Books by Bob and Penny Lord

THIS IS MY BODY, THIS IS MY BLOOD
Miracles of the Eucharist
THE MANY FACES OF MARY
a Love Story
WE CAME BACK TO JESUS
SAINTS AND OTHER POWERFUL WOMEN
IN THE CHURCH
SAINTS AND OTHER POWERFUL MEN
IN THE CHURCH
HEAVENLY ARMY OF ANGELS
SCANDAL OF THE CROSS
and Its Triumph
MARTYRS

ISBN 0-926143-12-3

Editor - Dr. Jeffrey Mirus, Trinity Communications

Photo Credits: Photos of the Basilica of the Rosary and
Shrine of Our Lady of Lourdes France
used with permission, Bureau de la Presse

Table of Contents

Bob and Penny Lord with Pope John II

Dedication
His Holiness, Pope John Paul II

In times of crisis, Our Lord fulfills His Promise that hell will not prevail against His Church, by sending us *Saints and other Powerful Men and Women in the Church*. Pope John Paul II is one of those men.

There is no person on earth whom we consider more an avid supporter of Our Lady, and the Rosary, than His Holiness, Pope John Paul II. Very possibly, he has been the greatest factor in bringing devotion to Our Lady and the Rosary back into the mainstream of the Catholic Church.

We have been very blessed to have been given the gift of this Pope by Our Lord Jesus and His Mother Mary. We believe Pope John Paul II is the most dynamic world leader, and the greatest pope in the history of the Church.

4

Bob and Penny Lord with Mother Angelica

Mother Mary Angelica

"Then I saw another Angel flying overhead, with everlasting Good News to announce to those who dwell on earth, to every nation, tribe, tongue and people" Rev 14:6

Mother Angelica is our earthly angel, who through Eternal Word Television Network, is fulfilling that prophecy in Holy Scripture. She has spread devotion to the Rosary to the four corners of this country, and now in the world.

We discovered the impact EWTN has had one day in March when a winter blizzard shut down EWTN for almost 24 hours. We received phone calls from all over the country; people in tears, sharing how they missed the Mass, praying the Rosary with EWTN, and our programs on Mother Mary.

I can just picture Jesus' Face, a hundred years from now, when He meets Mother Angelica at the gates of Heaven. He will smile at her and say, *"I've heard about you from My Mother. Please enter into My Kingdom."*

Always so few words to thank so many for working to bring about God's Will. As we give Retreats and speak at Conferences, more and more, the faithful recognize that we are only a *part* of a team of dedicated Catholic soldiers. To all in our Ministry who devote their time and pledge their loyalty, day after day, to their Church through our Ministry, to you who *live out* the Nicene Creed, our Pledge of Allegiance to our Pope and our Church, each day, this book is for you

And most especially to Brother Joseph and Luz Elena, to Lura and to all who slave in God's Vineyard, saying yes each day, so selflessly, it is your love for our Lord and His Mother, your love for us, as you have Journeyed in Faith with us, that has brought about not only this book but all the books we write. We salute you and thank you for your faith in the Mission our Lord has prepared for us.

To all our supporters, our Production Angels, who like the Widow in Holy Scripture, give very often from their substance, not from their excess; to the Pilgrims over the last ten years who have traveled with us to many of the Shrines we write about, thank you for walking beside us.

To all the faithful who read and buy our books, not only for yourselves but for your families, friends and Church, who spread the Good News by your grass roots evangelization, this book would not have come about without you. To the loyal subscribers of our *Good Newsletter* who affirm us with your letters, to "*fight the good fight*," you gave us the strength to write this book.

And lastly, but most importantly, we thank our family for sharing all our dreams and disappointments over the years, always there for us, standing beside us, encouraging us not only to go on, but to go beyond. May our Lord continue to hold you in the Palm of His Hand; we love you!

Introduction

Most of our television programs and videos have been inspired by a book or an article we have written. But in this instance, one of our television programs and videos was the catalyst for the writing of this book.

We had just returned from overseas where we had videotaped thirteen Documentaries on the "*Many Faces of Mary*" for Mother Angelica's Eternal Word Television Network. One of the "*Many Faces of Mary*" programs was videotaped in the Basilica of the Rosary at Lourdes. As the Rosary is such an integral part of Lourdes, we had decided to do a program meditating on the Life of Jesus and Mary using the fifteen chapels of the Rosary in the Basilica where Their Life is so poignantly portrayed.

We had just finished editing and were watching the finished product in our studio. The music, taken from the chanting of the pilgrims and priests during the Candlelight Procession every night, was taking us back to our very special time there. We were lost in our memories and in the Life of Our Savior and His Mother, when we looked up to see Lura standing there, mesmerized. Now Lura is a young girl, a convert of one year, who works in our Ministry and has become, in a short time, a part of us. We hadn't even heard her come into the editing suite. As she watched the program, tears welled up in her eyes. She blurted out, "*Oh, this is the most important program you have ever made.*" She had never learned anything about the Rosary in her RCIA program. She never knew why Catholics prayed the Rosary. Now, watching us share each of the Mysteries of the Rosary, she understood. Her next word was, "*Oh, if you would only write a book like that, it would help converts so much!*"

A few weeks, later, after the program had aired four times in one week, we began receiving phone calls from viewers. The thrust of the comments was, "*I thought I knew everything there was to know about the Rosary. Your program gave me new insights I had never dreamed of. Have you ever considered putting them down in book form?*"

Now, we have never believed in *coincidence*, unless it's *Holy Coincidence!* We do know that the Lord sometimes uses a 2x4 to get our attention. When we hear what we believe is the Lord speaking to us, we listen, and act on it. This was definitely one of those times. We felt that Our Lord was writing in blood and ink: "*Write reflections on My Life and that of My Mother using these beautiful Chapels, at the Basilica of the Rosary in Lourdes.*"

All who had seen the program said that the Chapels were such an inspiration while meditating on the Rosary. But now we knew that the Chapels had to be printed in full color in our book! We had photographed all the Chapels when we made our television program. We would use these photos for the book. We contacted the officials at Lourdes for permission. In the meantime, we were trying to determine if we could *afford* to print a book with fifteen photos in full color. As we tossed the cost versus the need back and forth, the Lord let us know, most clearly, during our time at the Blessed Sacrament Chapel, that He wanted us to print it in full color. We were also given the word that this book is a *meditation* book, to be used over and over again, every time the Rosary is prayed.

†

The Rosary is one of the most powerful gifts, Our Lady has ever given us. By praying the Rosary, we literally re-live the Life of the Son, through the eyes of the Mother; we truly "*Go to Jesus through Mary*".

How often, though, we don't take advantage of this most important prayer. We go through the Hail Marys, as if we're trying to beat the land-speed record. We lose our focus; our minds wander, thinking of everything but the matter at hand, the life of Jesus through His Mother Mary.

†

In the beginning, God carefully, lovingly created the world. The *Master Craftsman* left nothing out, not even the smallest detail. He knew what it took to make us happy on earth, and what would lead to misery and finally hell. He made a place of peace and order. We have only to look at the universe, and the anatomy of man, to begin to comprehend some of God's genius. After He was finished, God saw all the things *They*[1] had made and that they were very good. Everything God formed was *very good*.

God is Love! After He created the heavens and the earth, the creatures of the sea, the air and the land, He molded a man in His Image. Here, we see God as a Potter, excitedly taking the finest earth from the land that He had created and the purest water from the sea that He had created, and mixing the two together, lovingly forming man. After He looked at His creation, He was well pleased!

Again, sensitive to His creation's needs, He could see that the creatures of the earth were not enough for the man. He created a woman, taking her from the man's side. God first placed the man in a deep sleep. God did this so the man would feel no pain. Did He take the woman from the rib below the man's heart, the very spot where our Lord would be pierced by the centurion's sword?

God called the man Adam[2] and the man called the woman Eve. When Adam called the woman *Eve*, he, by this name which means *living*[3], declared her "*mother of the living*[4]".

---

[1]It is clear that by the use of the plural, we know that at the time of creation, it was the Trinity Who was involved. God the Father, God the Son and the Holy Spirit were there from the very beginning, as we profess in "the Glory be..."

[2]The Hebrew word meaning man

[3]Derived from the Hebrew word meaning "living".

We know that all went well, until the author of lies, the fallen Lucifer tempted the woman to disobey God. But, as the woman Eve was betraying God, He in His Mercy had already the *instrument* through which the Redeemer would come to save His people. He already had the new Eve in His Mind when He addressed the serpent.

"I will put enmities between you and the woman, and your seed and her seed; He shall crush your head, and you shall lie in wait for His heel.(Gn 3:15)"

She, Mary our *true* Mother, would be the instrument to undo what the first mother of the living did. No more, would the children of God be separated from Him. And Mother Mary has been stepping on the head of the enemy, for the last 2000 years.

†

We've dared to dream in this book about what might have been, in addition to what we know. In most areas, we have used Holy Scripture. In others, we've turned to the Tradition of the Church. Where there have been blank spaces, we have prayed for inspiration from the Holy Spirit. We pray we've given you some insights you may never had thought of before.

†

Our Community prays the fifteen decades of the Rosary every day. We start with good intentions to really walk with Jesus through the eyes of Mary. But while we are sincere, our humanity clicks in, and before long, we get lost on thoughts other than the Rosary. For our own concentration, and prayerfully, as an aid to you, in meditating on the Mysteries of the Rosary, we invite you to join us, as we peer into the heart of Mary, to discover what each of the Mysteries are saying to us, today. Come with us to Jesus, through His Most Magnificent Mother, Mary.

---

[4]Catholic Encyclopedia

Pope John Paul II - True Meaning of Holy Week

Each pilgrimage, we lead to Italy, always includes an audience with our Pope (when he is in Rome). When we brought pilgrims to Rome, years ago, we were not aware that His Holiness Pope John Paul II was *teaching* the audience, from what is now the *Universal Catechism*. Our Pope has been working on a catechism that will tell the whole truth, the *one* truth, according to the Magisterium and the Traditions of the Church (which are one and the same). Knowing that there can be only *one* truth, this has been of utmost urgency to him and to the Church. There has been much confusion on what is according to the Faith and what is someone's conjecture or hypothesis. Confusion is not of the Lord; Unity, being of *"one mind and one heart"* is, as we find in His Word.

Just as we were preparing to close the writing of our book: *"The Rosary, The Life of Jesus and Mary"*, what should we read, but the Pope's general audience of April 7th, 1993. He spoke on the last three days before Easter. Sometimes, in an effort to get to Easter, we pass too quickly over the time and the events that brought it all about. We were so moved by the passionate way our Pope spoke of the price our Lord paid for our Salvation and the purpose of those last three days of His Life, we had an urgency to share this with you. We believe that as you read this, you will understand what the Rosary is all about, and what our Church is all about.

†††

The Pope's Audience - April 7th, 1993

**"Holy Week is called 'holy'
because during this week the basic events
of the Christian religion are commemorated;
the institution of the Eucharist,
Jesus' Passion and Death on the Cross,
and the Redeemer's glorious Resurrection"**

Dear Brothers and Sisters,

At the end of Lent, Holy Week brings us immediately to the feast of Easter, and is called *"Holy"* precisely because during this week the basic events of the Christian religion are commemorated; the institution of the Eucharist, Jesus' Passion and Death on the Cross, and the Redeemer's glorious Resurrection.

During the Sacred Triduum,[1] therefore, we are invited to meditate on and live with deepest fervor the *"central mystery of salvation"* by participating in the solemn liturgical celebration which enables us to **relive the final days of Jesus' life**. For every person they have a lasting essential value.

Holy Thursday takes us back to the institution of the Eucharist, the supreme Gift of God's Love in His plan of redemption. During the Supper that evening, Jesus mystically anticipated the sacrifice of Calvary and gave Himself in sacrifice under the appearance of bread and wine, as he Himself had foretold[2] and entrusted to the Apostles and their successors the mission and power of perpetuating its memory by repeating the same rite: *"Do this in memory of Me!"*

---

[1] Sacred Triduum- the three days of prayer preparing for the Feast of Easter.

[2] John 6

Writing to the Corinthians around A.D. 53-56, the Apostle Paul strengthened the first Christians in the truth of the *"Eucharistic mystery"* by sharing with them what he himself had learned:

"For I received from the Lord what I also handed down to you, that the Lord Jesus, on the night He was handed over, took bread, and, after He had given thanks, broke it and said, 'This is My Body that is for you. Do this in memory of Me.' In the same way also the cup, after supper, saying, 'This cup is the new covenant in My Blood. Do this, as often as you drink It, in remembrance of Me."[3]

Words of fundamental importance! They recall what Jesus did at the Last Supper; they proclaim to us the *"sacrificial"* intention of bread and wine, replacing the sacrificial lamb of the Jews, and His express intention to make the Apostles and their successors the ministers of the Eucharist.

"What Jesus did at the Last Supper was to proclaim to us the 'sacrificial intention' of bread and wine, replacing the sacrificial lamb of the Jews, and His express intention to make the Apostles and their successors the ministers of the Eucharist."

The Eucharist, as Christ's Real Presence and as the Sacrament of interior communion of love and salvation; the priesthood, as the eucharistic ministry reserved to the Apostles and their successors; This is the essential meaning of Holy Thursday. It is a question of a *"dogma of faith,"* to be accepted then with deep, abiding gratitude. It means Christ's Gift, to be increasingly appreciated in an attitude of sincere, intense devotion.

St. Paul warns the faithful of Corinth: *"Therefore whoever eats the Bread or drinks the cup of the Lord unworthily*

---

[3] 1 Cor. 11:23-25

will have to answer for the Body and the Blood of the Lord. A person should examine himself, and so eat the Bread and drink the cup. For anyone who eats and drinks without discerning the Body, eats and drinks judgment on himself."[4]

Thursday, the first day of the Sacred Triduum, is also an excellent occasion to pray for priests that they may always correspond to their dignity, since their life is totally consecrated to the Eucharist.

"Good Friday makes us relive the 'sorrowful mystery' of Jesus' Passion, and death on the Cross."

Good Friday makes us relive the "sorrowful mystery" of Jesus' Passion, and death on the Cross.

In relation to the Crucified, the words He spoke at the Last Supper take on dramatic import: "This is My Blood of the new covenant, which will be shed for many, for the forgiveness of sins."[5]

Jesus wanted to offer His Life in sacrifice for the forgiveness of humanity's sins. To accomplish this He chose crucifixion, the cruelest and most humiliating death. St. Peter regards it this way in his First Letter: Jesus *"Himself bore our sins in His Body upon the Cross, so that, free from sin, we might live for righteousness. By His Wounds you have been healed."*[6]

And several times St. Paul stresses that *"Christ died for our sins in accordance with the Scriptures"*,[7] *"Christ loved us and handed Himself over for us as a sacrificial offering"*,[8] *"For there is one God. There is also one Mediator between God and*

---

[4] 1 Cor. 11:27-29
[5] Mark 14:24; Matt 26:28; Luke 22:20
[6] Peter 2:24-25
[7] 1 Cor. 15:3
[8] Eph. 5:22

men, the man Christ Jesus, Who gave Himself as ransom for all."[9]

As with the Eucharist, so too with Jesus' Passion and Death on the Cross, the mystery becomes vast and unfathomable for human reason. Inasmuch as He is true man, the Messiah indeed suffered unspeakably, from the spiritual agony in Gethsemane to the long, dreadful agony on the Cross. The way to Calvary was one of indescribable suffering, leading to the frightful torture of crucifixion. What a mystery is Christ's Passion: God made man suffer to save man, taking upon Himself all the tragedy of humanity.

"The way to Calvary was one of indescribable suffering, leading to the frightful torture of crucifixion."

Good Friday, therefore, brings to mind the continuous succession of historical trials, the human events marked by the perennial struggle between good and evil. The Cross is truly the scale of history: It is understood only by meditating on and loving the Crucified.

St. John wrote: *"In this is love, not that we have loved God, but that He has loved us and sent His Son as expiation for our sins"*;[10] and so St. Paul asserted: *"God proves His Love for us that while we were still sinners Christ died for us."*[11]

In His plan of salvation and sanctification, God does not follow our ways: He undergoes the Cross to reach His glorification, thus spurring us to patience and confidence. Dear brothers and sisters, let us learn from Good Friday to accompany Jesus on His way of sorrow, with humility, trust and abandonment to the Will of God, finding support and comfort amidst the sufferings of life in the Cross of Christ.

---

[9] 1 Tim. 2:5-6
[10] 1 John 4:10
[11] Rom. 5:8

"God does not follow our ways:
He undergoes the Cross to reach His glorification."

The Sacred Triduum concludes with the radiant *"glorious mystery"* of Christ's Resurrection. He had foretold: *"On the third day I shall rise again!"*

It is the definitive victory of life over death. Jesus will appear after His Resurrection to Mary Magdalen, to the devoted women, to the Apostles, and then to the disciples. He will show them the marks of the Crucifixion on His Body. He will let them touch His Person. He will eat with the Apostles and allow then to experience the wonderful newness of His glorified Body.

For believers the Resurrection is the final definitive guarantee of Christ's Divinity, because of which they are called to believe in His Word with absolute certitude.

In the mysterious silence of Holy Saturday, as we prepare for the Holy Vigil in which we commemorate the light of salvation breaking through the darkness, our heart contemplates God's marvels, the *magnalia Dei*, culminating in the Solemnity of Easter, the center and fulcrum[12] of the Christian people's life.

Dear brothers and sisters, may Mary most holy, who stood erect beneath the Cross as Jesus suffered and died, herself grieving but calm and confident, accompany us in meditation during the Sacred Triduum and lead us to experience the renewing joy of Easter.

With my blessing and cordial best wishes to all!

†††

(Reprinted from *L'Osservatore Romano*, English language edition, April 14, 1993)

---

[12] Fulcrum in Webster's dictionary: 1.base, beam, support or point of support on which a lever turns in raising or moving something.

The First Joyful Mystery

The Second Joyful Mystery

The Third Joyful Mystery

LVMEN AD REVELATIONEM GENTIVM

The Fourth Joyful Mystery

The Fifth Joyful Mystery

The First Sorrowful Mystery

The Second Sorrowful Mystery

The Third Sorrowful Mystery

The Fourth Sorrowful Mystery

The Fifth Sorrowful Mystery

The First Glorious Mystery

The Second Glorious Mystery

The Third Glorious Mystery

The Fourth Glorious Mystery

The Fifth Glorious Mystery

Our Lady of Lourdes

How to Pray the Rosary

On Monday and Thursday, pray the Joyful Mysteries; Tuesday and Friday, the Sorrowful; Wednesday, Saturday and Sunday, the Glorious; or say all 15 decades each day.

1. Make the *Sign of the Cross*.
2. Recite the *"Apostles Creed"*. (holding the Crucifix)
3. Recite the *"Our Father"*.   (Large Bead)
4. Recite 3 *"Hail Marys"*.   (Small Beads)
5. Recite the *"Glory Be to the Father"*.
6. Say **Fatima Prayer** and **Short Prayer to Mary** (optional)
7. Announce the First Mystery of the Joyful Mysteries
8. Recite the *"Our Father"*. (Large Bead)
9. Say 10 *"Hail Marys"* (Small Beads)
10. Recite the *"Glory Be to the Father"*.
11. Then pray the **Fatima Prayer** (optional)
12. Then pray **a Short Prayer to Mary** (optional)
13. Announce the Second Mystery of The Joyful Mysteries
14. Repeat 7-8-9-10-11-12
15. Then repeat the same prayers as you meditate on all the *Joyful*, the *Sorrowful*, and the *Glorious Mysteries*.
16. After the five (or fifteen) decades are finished,
    Pray the **Hail Holy Queen**
17. Pray the **Memorare**
18. V. Pray for us, O Holy Mother of God
    R. That we maybe worthy of the promises of Christ.

LET US PRAY

O God, Whose only-begotten Son, by His life, death and Resurrection has purchased for us the rewards of eternal life, grant we beseech Thee, that meditating upon these Mysteries of the Most Holy Rosary of the Virgin Mary, we may imitate what they contain and obtain what they promise, through the same Christ our Lord.   Amen.

Prayers of the Holy Rosary

THE SIGN OF THE CROSS

"In the Name of the Father, and of the Son, and of the Holy Spirit, Amen."

THE APOSTLES' CREED

"I believe in God the Father Almighty, Creator of Heaven and earth; and in Jesus Christ, His only Son, our Lord; Who was conceived by the Holy Spirit; born of the Virgin Mary; suffered under Pontius Pilate; was crucified, died and was buried; He descended into hell; the third day He arose again from the dead; He ascended into Heaven; sitteth at the right hand of God the Father Almighty; from thence He shall come to judge the living and the dead.
I believe in the Holy Spirit; the Holy Catholic Church; the Communion of Saints; the forgiveness of sins; the Resurrection of the body; and life everlasting. Amen."

THE OUR FATHER

"Our Father, Who art in Heaven; hallowed by Thy Name; Thy kingdom come; Thy will be done on earth as it is in Heaven. Give us this day our daily bread; and forgive us our trespasses as we forgive those who trespass against us, and lead us not into temptation; but deliver us from evil. Amen."

THE HAIL MARY

"Hail Mary, full of grace, the Lord is with thee; blessed art thou among women, and blessed is the fruit of thy womb, Jesus. Holy Mary, Mother of God, pray for us sinners, now and at the hour of our death. Amen."

THE GLORY BE TO THE FATHER

"Glory be to the Father, and to the Son, and to the Holy Spirit. As it was in the beginning, is now, and ever shall be, world without end. Amen."

THE FATIMA PRAYER

"Oh my Jesus, forgive us our sins; save us from the fires of hell. Lead all souls into Heaven, especially those in most need of Thy mercy."

A SHORT PRAYER TO MARY

"Our Lady of Lourdes, pray for us, or *Our Lady of Fatima, pray for us,* or *Our Lady of Guadalupe, pray for us,* or *Our Lady of Czestochowa, pray for us,* etc
any other title of Our Lady you would like to use"

THE HAIL HOLY QUEEN

"Hail, Holy Queen, Mother of Mercy, our life, our sweetness, and our hope. To thee we cry, poor banished children of Eve! To thee do we send up our sighs; mourning and weeping in this vale of tears! Turn then, most gracious Advocate, thine eyes of mercy towards us; and after this, our exile, show unto us the blessed fruit of thy Womb, Jesus.
O Clement, O loving, O sweet Virgin Mary.
Pray for us, O Holy Mother of God
That we may be worthy of the promises of Christ."

THE MEMORARE

Remember, O most gracious Virgin Mary
that never was it known that anyone who fled to thy protection, implored thy help, or sought thy intercession was left unaided.
Inspired by this confidence I fly unto thee O Virgin of Virgins, my Mother.
To thee, I come; before thee I stand, sinful and sorrowful.
O Mother of the Word Incarnate, despise not my petitions, but in thy mercy hear and answer me. **AMEN**

The Annunciation

This day, that would change the history of the world, started like any other day. But the people of Israel could feel an electricity in the air that cut through the calm of the day. Mary had grown up with a full knowledge of Holy Scripture. She, like her brothers and sisters of Israel, was awaiting the Messiah. This promise of a Redeemer had been given to the Jewish people *before* Moses led them out of the desert.

There was a great need for the Messiah. The chosen people had suffered for many centuries, rather than give homage to false gods. They were enslaved and persecuted before, but now, the Romans had completely crushed them. The worst part of their captivity was not the slavery of their bodies, but the enslavement of their souls. Their ancestors had died rather than worship pagan gods. Now, what could not be done with the use of force, was being accomplished by the pervading, insidious influence of their captors. More and more, the Romans' godless philosophy infused them, choking out the beliefs and traditions of the sons of David. All that the Jewish people had left were *memories* of King David and King Solomon. They needed another David, another Solomon, someone who would deliver them from their enemies, and give them back their faith and their hope.

It was into this setting that Mary was born and grew up. She grieved for her people, not so much because of their physical suffering, but because they were losing their heritage, their faith in Yahweh, Abba, their Father, their trust that He would take care of them. They were looking to *man* for answers, and Mary knew there would be no help coming from man. She prayed that her people would look to their God for deliverance, trusting that He would hear and answer them.

Mary's life was one of prayer

Mary had been consecrated to the Temple, as a child. Her ongoing prayer was that the Messiah would come in her lifetime and free the people she loved so much. She spent much of her time in the Temple; but since her father's death, she spent a great deal of time caring for her aging mother, Anne. Mary prayed constantly, even while doing her chores at home. There was a saying: "*What good can come out of Nazareth.*"[1] Nazareth, through the will of God would give us Mother Mary, Saint Joseph and Jesus.

It was late afternoon. March was filled with promise of new beginnings. Mary had a spring to her step, as she walked home from the well, from which she drew water each day. But somehow, this day felt different. Was she remembering the ancient prayer said at the Seder (the meal celebrating the Passover): "*Why is this night different from any other night?*" At the Seder, there was always an extra place set at the table in expectation of Elijah's return. But, this night, the place set was beneath Mary's heart, and *it* would be filled by the Messiah!

Let us try to envision how the events might have taken place. The sun went down, and dusk began to dim the sky; a chill crept into the air. Mary was kneeling in her home, lost in prayer. She began to wonder how it would be, when the Messiah arrived. We can see her praying, a cool breeze brushing past her. Was it the winds blowing off the sea, cooling the house? There was a tingling electricity in the air, a fluttering sound, like that of birds' wings. She looked around. There was nothing. Suddenly a great calm came over her. The wind stopped. There was a hush, a stillness, as if time had stopped. A figure of a beautiful young man entered through the window. There was a brightness about him, as if he were translucent. He looked at her. His eyes

---

[1]John:1:46

were brilliant. At first, she was frightened; then a rush of warmth and peace came over her whole body. She couldn't take her eyes from him.

The Angel said to her, "*Hail, most favored one. The Lord is with you.*"[2]

She was startled by his words.

"*Do not be afraid, Mary; you have found favor with the Lord. You will conceive in your womb, and bear a Child, and you will call Him Jesus. He will be great, and will be called the Son of the Most High, and the Lord God will give to Him the throne of David His father, and He will reign over the House of Jacob forever, and His Kingdom will have no end.*"[3]

What was he talking about? How could she conceive and bear a child? She was a virgin. She wasn't married! She was engaged to Joseph the carpenter, but they had vowed to live a celibate life when they became husband and wife. Yet while she wondered, she never doubted. She asked him with excitement and awe. It was the way a trusting child might ask her daddy how an impossible task would be accomplished.

"*How can this be, since I am a virgin?*"[4]

The Angel answered her, "*The Holy Spirit will come upon you and the power of the Most High will overshadow you and for that reason the Holy Child to be born will be called the Son of God*".[5]

She gasped. It was as if she was almost afraid to breathe. She didn't understand, at that moment, what the messenger meant by the Holy Spirit coming upon her. The key word in her mind, in her entire being, was "*The Son of God*". Is this Angel speaking of the Messiah? Is he telling

---

[2]Luke 1:28
[3]Luke 1:30
[4]Luke 1:34
[5]Luke 1:35

me I am to be the mother of the Messiah, the Son of God? Am I the one, I've been praying for, the one to be the vessel to bring salvation into the world? Is that what he's saying? Mary knew that the Messiah would be born of a virgin. It was part of Holy Scripture. But, she never dared to think *she* would be the one. Her prayer had been that the Messiah would be born in her generation and she might *serve* the mother of the Messiah.

The Angel further affirmed the power of God. He added:

"And behold, your cousin Elizabeth in her old age has also conceived a son; she is in her sixth month, and everyone thought she was barren. You see, with God, nothing is impossible."[6]

Mary silently prayed: "Oh, my Lord, it *is* You! Is this really possible? Would You give this honor to me? I'm not worthy." But the words of the Angel pierced her senses, opening her heart and mind: *"You see, with God, nothing is impossible."* She responded, in her heart: "I trust You, my Lord and my God. I know You would never hurt me. And I would give up my life for You."

She looked up at the Angel before her. He was waiting for something, what? Was this messenger of God waiting for an answer from her? She looked at him, again. He *was* waiting for her *yes!* Tears streamed down her face. He looked at her with so much love. His gaze filled her with a profound warmth. She gave her answer:

"I am the handmaiden of the Lord. Let it be done unto me according to your word."[7] And as the tears cascaded down her cheeks, she cried out in her heart, *"Yes! I say Yes!"*

Could she hear the choirs of Angels singing praises to the Lord, at these words of their future Queen? The Angel

---

[6]Luke 1:36-37
[7]Luke 1:38

before her, whom we know to be Gabriel, looked at her with blinding joy in his eyes. A brilliant light filled the room, and surrounded her. She felt a surge of energy go through her. She looked up at the Angel. He looked at her. He smiled. It was done.

The Angel slowly disappeared, and the room became dark. The girl, now woman, sat in the darkness, her heart beating, her mind racing. She repeated silently, the words of the Angel. She was to be the Mother of God. She could feel His Presence inside her. It was true. Now she understood!

But do we understand? *Incarnation came about!* This is one the holiest moments in Salvation History, when through the *yes* of Mary, God became God-Man, and Heaven was joined with earth. During the Nicene Creed, at Holy Mass, after we profess *"For us men and our salvation He came down from Heaven"*, we reverently add *"By the power of the Holy Spirit He was born of the Virgin Mary, and became man."* This moment is so holy that we are directed in the Missalette to bow, and reflect on what happened in a little house in Nazareth, to a Virgin named Mary; and *then* go on to recite the rest of the Nicene Creed. This is the moment when God finalized His Plan, begun in the Garden of Eden, for a virgin to give birth to the new Adam Who *"will strike at his head."*[8] At this moment, the Salvation of man began, and so we bow in adoration. At Christmas time, we kneel in reverence. The next time we kneel is on *Good Friday*, when our Lord gives up His Spirit on the Cross. It has been completed. What began in the womb of our most precious Mother Mary ended with her under the Cross, her Baby Who was born to be sacrificed, dying for our sins. Next Holy Mass, will you bow; will you genuflect?

We know and believe that Mary was Immaculately Conceived. She never bore the sin of Adam, but it didn't

---

[8]Gen 3:15

mean she was exempt from temptation. After Gabriel the Archangel left her, did the evil one try to fill her mind with fear? Mary was with Child, without a husband. Who was going to accept, she had conceived through the Holy Spirit? What would the townspeople say? She knew what they would do. Do you have any idea what they did with pregnant, unmarried women in that day and age? *They stoned them to death!* How could she explain what had happened to her mother? *What was she going to say to Joseph?*

It's pretty well accepted that Mary was in her teen years. Given this set of circumstances, who would have the courage to share what had happened? Did this go through Mary's mind, when the reality of what had happened came crashing down on her? She had said yes; she was now with Child. She had a heavy burden to carry; but the Lord gave her the strength and courage to handle it.

God doesn't make mistakes. He knew right from the beginning that her Child would be the One to bring mankind from condemnation (through Adam) to Salvation (through the New Adam - Jesus). As Eve the first mother of mankind was betraying the trust that God had placed in her and Adam, God our Father was already raising up a new Eve, one who would step on the head of the serpent who had tricked God's first creations to sin against Him. Through a Virgin's yes to God, mankind would rise from the fall caused by one woman (Eve), to New Life through another. And Mary was now coming to terms that she was to be that instrument.

Mary was the happiest woman in the world. She was highly favored of the Lord. Her *Magnificat*, which she will proclaim a few weeks, later, in the presence of her cousin Elizabeth, will confirm the overflowing love and trust she had for her God, Who had blessed her so.

But it wasn't going to be all roses. There was that problem of *how* to tell what had happened, especially to her mother Anne and her betrothed Joseph. We have to believe that Anne knew that Mary, her child, had been born for specialness. With a mother's knowing heart, we are sure Anne believed Mary's account of what had happened to her, *immediately*. Mary had never been anything but pure and holy.

Then there was Joseph. Mary had to tell Joseph! She loved him, dearly. Although it is believed by some, he was older than she, there was a bond between them that was strong. He had always trusted her, completely. Now, she looked deeply into his eyes, as she explained the events of the Annunciation. He was sad; he was hurt; he didn't believe her. What wounded Mary most, having hurt Joseph, or the fact that he didn't believe her? How do you feel when someone you love very much, your very best friend, doesn't believe you? It's devastating. It must have been that way for Mary.

But she persevered. She trusted in her God. She knew, He would not abandon her. After all she now bore the Son of the God in her womb. As much as she grieved, seeing Joseph suffer pain and sorrow, she couldn't help but be so happy when she felt the warm glow of the Messiah Who was growing inside her.

The Lord intervened, as she trusted He would. An Angel came to Joseph in a dream, and confirmed Mary's story. He told Joseph, it was all right to take Mary as his wife. We know that Joseph was relieved. He loved Mary. How could he help but love her. With the exception of her Son, she was the most perfect human being the world would ever know.

These are the Joyful Mysteries of the Rosary. They are happy times. But they're intermingled with some extremely difficult times, as well. It was not easy for Mary, explaining her situation. Scripture leaves a lot unsaid about what transpired between Joseph and Mary. But we do know that Joseph was going to have Mary put away privately.[9] Nothing *she* said could convince him that she was telling the truth. It took an Angel's intercession to finally make Joseph believe what Mary was saying. How did she endure those days or weeks in between? What kind of a strain was put on Mary, and how did she react to it?

There are many teachings, we can draw from the great Fiat of Mary. What was she doing when the Angel Gabriel appeared to her? We believe she was praying! What had been the focus of her life? Getting to know the Lord, her God, by studying Holy Scripture and following the traditions of her Faith. She *knew* this man was an Angel! After all, she had spent her life learning about how God had spoken to His chosen people through the Prophets and the *Angels*.

We are often asked how we know, it is God speaking to us. Where is your heart? That is where your treasure will be. If you are looking down, spending most of your time and energy on passing things of this world, then this is what you will know. And the messenger, you will recognize and give your yes to, is not one from *Above*, but below. Mary's vision went heavenward to the Father and His promise to His people.

The Angel Gabriel spoke to a heart whose every beat was in joyful anticipation of the Messiah. Mary was preparing for her Lord's coming, and He came and made a dwelling place in her. He came and she became a walking tabernacle bringing Jesus to everyone she encountered. Do we prepare before Mass for the Messiah Who is to come, Our Lord Jesus, present to us Body, Blood, Soul and Divinity? As we await Our Lord, do we consecrate to Him: our thoughts, our eyes, our ears, our arms and legs, our

---

[9]Matthew 1:19 Joseph did not want any harm to come to Mary.

heart?   Do we reverently carry Him and His Love to everyone we meet?   Do they see Jesus in us, as Elizabeth did in Mary, in the Visitation?   Are we changed by Communion with the Lord through His Eucharist, as well as through Him in the Word?   Who do they see, when they look at you?

Could it be our fault that our brothers and sisters do not know who Mother Mary is?   *Do we share* with them the scripture passage that tells us how the Holy Spirit descended upon Mary and, through Him, she conceived the Lord, our Savior?   *Do we tell them*, she was with the Apostles on the Day of Pentecost, when the Holy Spirit descended upon them, giving them the courage to die Martyrs' deaths for the Faith?   *Who is guilty*, they who love the Holy Spirit and say that they are filled with Him, and do not recognize Mother Mary or we who fail to share the Mother, Jesus entrusted to all of us?

†

The overpowering message for us in the Annunciation is Mary's *"Yes!"*   The Lord gave her an impossible (for man) proposition, and she said "Yes".   She had faith in God that no matter what happened, He would make it right.   She could stand on that faith.   She staked her life on it.   Do we trust God in proportions anywhere near those of Mary?   Do we give over control to Him, and then take it back at the first sign of adversity?   Or do we cling to control over our lives until we get into a problem situation we just can't handle, and then turn to God for help?

Mary didn't say very much in Scripture; but every word out of her mouth was a gem.   If we were to sum up the teaching of the Annunciation, words to live by, it would be those of Mary,

"Let it be done unto me according to Your Word."

The Visitation

"My Soul magnifies the Lord
and my spirit rejoices in God my Savior"

Reflecting on the Second Joyful Mystery of the Rosary, the little virgin from Nazareth begins to grow overwhelmingly in our eyes. We see the *obedience* of Mary! At the Annunciation, recognizing the Angel as a messenger of God, she had said yes to bearing the Son of God. When the Angel Gabriel told her that her cousin Elizabeth was with child, she *trusted* in his word knowing he was from God. Because she, like the other people of Israel, had been preparing for the Messiah, and had studied the Word, she knew the Lord would have wanted her to go and serve her cousin; and so she *obeyed*, once more. As we walk through the rose petals that make up the Rosary, we will encounter the many times Mary obeyed. As we learn more about Jesus, we realize that His Life was our path to Heaven. As you walk with Mary, you will discover she knows the way.

We see the *selflessness* of Mary in action. Her choice to be for her cousin Elizabeth during her pregnancy, shows an unconditional caring for others, that we've only seen in One other Person in the history of the world, her Son Jesus.

But, there was something else. Although there was a *familial* bond between Mary and her cousin Elizabeth, we believe there was another bond, which had been molded in Heaven. The plan to have the Angel tell Mary of her cousin's pregnancy had to begin in Heaven. Can we not see God formulating His plan? The son of Elizabeth would be the one who would herald the Messiah, the Son of Mary, into the world.

Neither of these women should have been pregnant. Mary was a virgin; Elizabeth was barren. There had to be a *Heavenly* connection between them. Is this why the Angel told Mary about her cousin being *"with child"*? Did the Lord want her to go and serve her cousin Elizabeth? Were she and Elizabeth part of a particular plan of the Father's? Had an Angel told Elizabeth, when she conceived, that her child would be special, too? Were these things going through Mary's mind, as she proceeded on her appointed mission?

When we see statues or paintings of Mary, for the most part, they depict a very delicate, almost dresden-like Mary. And I am sure, she had all those qualities. But Mother Mary was also *strong*! We will see, as we journey in faith with her and her Son through the Rosary, how very strong she was. The trip from Nazareth to Ein Karem, where Elizabeth and Zechariah lived, was long and dangerous. Mary had to travel through the mountains of Judea, past Jerusalem. Today, it is a challenge. In the time of Jesus and Mary, with dirt roads, cut out by people travelling by donkey or by foot, it had to be hazardous for someone with child. But Mary did not think, for one moment, about her comfort. The Angel had told her of her cousin's need and she said *yes*, one more time.

There was a radiance about Mary as she travelled to her cousin's house. The words of the Angel echoed in her soul:

"Do not fear, Mary. You have found favor with God. You shall conceive and bear a Son and give Him the name Jesus.....He will rule over the house of Jacob forever, and His reign will have no end....The Holy Spirit will come upon you, and the Power of the Most High will overshadow you; hence, the holy offspring to be born will be called Son of God." (Luke 1:30)

Mary proceeded, in haste, to fulfill the Angel's command, never once looking back. The Angel had told her not to be afraid.[1] And she trusted his message, knowing it was from the Lord. Mary *believed*, the Lord would take care of her and her unborn Child. She knew that the Child she was carrying, had the special protection of the Father's *"Heavenly Army of Angels."*[2] What then was there to fear?

Son of God! She couldn't get these words out of her mind. Her senses reeled at the thought. She was to be the mother of the Son of God. It was incredible! She was carrying God inside her body. What would He be like? How would their life together, be?

As soon as Elizabeth saw her, *"the baby leapt in her womb. She was filled with the Holy Spirit."* This was to fulfill the prophecy the Angel Gabriel gave to Zechariah,

"...and he will be filled with the Holy Spirit from his mother's womb." [3]

Tradition tells us that, at this meeting with Jesus, while both were still in their mothers' wombs, John was freed from *original sin*. While he was conceived with sin, we are told he was born without sin.

There was immediate recognition between the two unborn babies, John and Jesus. A bond between the two children, conceived in Heaven before the dawn of creation, was *affirmed* at this meeting, and further *confirmed* at the Jordan River some thirty years later. Thus did Jesus say of John, *"In truth I tell you, of all the children born to women, there has never been anyone greater than John the Baptist."*[4]

A similar bond was forged between Mary and Elizabeth. The skies opened; the brilliance of the Holy Spirit descended on both women. It was as if Mary and Elizabeth

---

[1]In Holy Scripture, the Lord tells us not to be afraid 365 times, once for every day of our year.

[2]For more about the Angels and their place in the life of Jesus and Mary, read Bob and Penny Lord's book: *"Heavenly Army of Angels"*.

[3]Luke 1:15

[4]Matt 11:11

were given total knowledge of God's plan, through the movement of the Spirit. Whatever had not been revealed to them before, suddenly became crystal clear. Elizabeth cried out in a loud voice:

"Blest are you among women and blest is the fruit of your womb. But who am I that the mother of my Lord should come to me? The moment your greeting sounded in my ears, the baby leapt in my womb for joy. Blest is she who trusted that the Lord's words to her would be fulfilled."[5]

There is so much in this statement of Elizabeth's. Scripture scholars tell us that Elizabeth's meaning in her first sentence was: *"Blest are you among women"* **because** *"blest is the Fruit of your womb"*. With this declaration, Elizabeth prophesied Mary's future role in the world, and in the Church, that Mary would be blessed among all women. It is true that Mary said *yes* to the Angel Gabriel. **But, it was by the Fruit of her womb, she was blessed among all women.** Mother Mary will tell you that, of herself, she is nothing. She always points to her Son. She is the intercessor to her *Son*; she is not the One Who brings about miracles, Who heals, Who forgives, Who gives us life. She points to her Son. A priest once said, *"What did Mother Mary do? She stood there and allowed the Holy Spirit to fill her. And because of this, the world will never be the same."* One name that our Mother appeared under, was *"Our Lady of Hope"*.[6] She is our Mother who turns to her Son Jesus, and through His love for her, we have *hope* that He will give us another chance. Like Abraham and Moses, she is always asking for another chance for her children, you and me.

---

[5]Luke 1:42-45

[6]Our Lady of Pontmain, France is known as *Our Lady of Hope*. More about this apparition and others that our Lady has made, are in Bob and Penny Lord's book: *The Many Faces of Mary, a love story*.

Mary was blessed because of the *Fruit* she carried within her, under her heart. Do you think blessedness is impossible for you and me? Do we not carry the *Fruit* of Mary's womb under our heart after we have received the Eucharist? After the Holy Spirit hovered over Mary and she conceived the Lord, change came about. Mary felt it; Elizabeth saw it; Mary was in *Communion* with the Lord within her. At Mass, the Holy Spirit descends upon bread and wine, and through the Priest's anointed hands, the Lord comes to us; He comes to be in *Communion* with us through His Body, Blood, Soul and Divinity. And a bond is made between us and the Fruit of Mary's womb.

Elizabeth was the very first human to call Mary the Mother of God: "*But who am I that the Mother of my Lord should come to me?*" She knew! This could not have come from human reasoning; only the Holy Spirit could have given her this wisdom. Mary's heart must have jumped when she heard those words. But think of it, for the last 2000 years, the Mother of God has been coming to us, through her apparitions. Do we ask with Elizabeth: "*But who am I that the Mother of my Lord should come to me?*"

Mary visited Elizabeth because the Angel Gabriel told her Elizabeth was with child. Elizabeth needed Mary and she responded to that need. Mother Mary has been responding to our needs for 2000 years. Do we, as Elizabeth, before us, accept the love and compassion of our Lady? Do we recognize her and revere her as the Mother of God? Do we defend her when she is maligned? Is she our Mother? In Guadalupe, she said: "*Am I not here who am your Mother?*" Well, is she our Mother? Do we share her with those who do not know who she is? Or are we afraid of what they will think? Are we more polite than holy?

The next words, we hear in Holy Scripture, are a confirmation of the Angel's words to Mary, "*Blest is she who*

trusted that the Lord's words to her would be fulfilled."[7]
Elizabeth *confirmed*, the Son of God was present in Mary's
womb. Everything the Angel had told Mary had come to
pass. Elizabeth knew all about it. Mary's soul soared to the
heights of Heaven. She was filled beyond the boundaries of
humanity. Her face flushed; her eyes beamed. Every part of
her body was raised heavenward. She proclaimed her
Magnificat. We are gifted to see the full blown image of
Mary, filled with the Holy Spirit, as she proclaims in words,
what has been in her heart, bursting to come out. With
Mary, we proclaim her Magnificat:

"My soul magnifies the Lord
and my spirit rejoices in God my Savior
For He has regarded the lowliness of His handmaid;
Behold, henceforth, all generations shall call me
blessed;
For He who is Mighty has done great things for me,
and Holy is His Name;
His mercy is from generation to generation
on those who fear Him.
He has shown might with His Arm,
He has scattered the proud in the deceit of their heart,
He has put down the mighty from their thrones,
and has exalted the lowly.
He has filled the hungry with good things,
and the rich He has sent away empty.
He has received Israel, His servant,
being mindful of His mercy.
Even as He spoke to our fathers,
To Abraham and his descendants forever."[8]

We can visualize the Angels surrounding Mary, their
Queen, as she made her pronouncement, guarding her,

---

[7]Luke 1:45
[8]Luke 1:46-55

hugging her with their wings, loving her. If we look with the eyes of the heart and not the head, we can experience the power and joy of the Holy Spirit encompassing the entire room. Did Mary turn to Elizabeth? Were their eyes filled with tears of joy? Did they embrace each other, knowingly? Did choirs of Angels sing praises to God, with this proclamation of Mary, Daughter of the Father, Spouse of the Holy Spirit, and Mother of the Savior of the world?

In Mary's Magnificat, we see an explosion of total acceptance of the powerful role the Lord is playing in her life, not only for her, but for all mankind. Most likely, these things had been building up in her mind and heart from the time the Angel came to her. But when Elizabeth affirmed what only Mary had known until that time, it had to come out. She couldn't hold it in any longer. She had to put to words, what was burning inside her. Her Magnificat was a *Canticle of Thanksgiving*. There was wisdom in every word she spoke, a wisdom only God could have given her. She acknowledged that God and *His* Gifts to her.

Mary stayed with Elizabeth for three months. Roles were reversed. The Mary that Elizabeth had known was the child of her sister Anne's old age. They were generations apart. Elizabeth could have been Mary's mother many times over. Mary had been the child consecrated to the Temple. But the minute Elizabeth saw her, she knew this was no longer a child, but a woman specially blessed. Elizabeth wanted to wait on Mary. But Mary had come for a purpose, to serve her cousin. It reminds us of Jesus, washing the feet of His disciples at the Last Supper. He was the Master; but He insisted on serving. Like Jesus, Mary set the example.

Let us ponder the possibilities, what might have happened, during that time they spent together. There was much joy in Mary at this time. She could be free with her cousin. Elizabeth knew who she was, and what the Lord was doing in her life. Mary could talk to her about it. They could dream together about the roles both their children would play in the salvation of Israel. Both women spent much of this time reading Scripture. Every time, they came across passages that referred to their children, their hearts abounded with joy. But the joy had to be mixed with sadness and apprehension when they read how the Messiah would have to suffer. At these times, did Elizabeth comfort Mary? Little did Elizabeth know that *her* son would have to die, because he was calling the world to repentance. Did Elizabeth remind Mary that God would give her strength for the years ahead, that He would take care of everything? *Mary trusted in the Lord!* She knew He would give her the graces she needed, for whatever she had to face.

Mary remained with Elizabeth until John the Baptist was born. We can see Mary holding the infant John in her arms. As she caressed his sweet face, did she look into this baby's soul? Could she envision what role he would have in her own Son's life? She thought of the words, the Angel spoke to Zechariah, regarding John the Baptist:

"Do not be frightened, Zechariah; your prayer has been heard. Your wife Elizabeth shall bear a son whom you shall call John. Joy and gladness will be yours, and many will rejoice at his birth; for he will be great in the Eyes of the Lord...he will be filled with the Holy Spirit from his mother's womb. Many sons of Israel, he will bring back to the Lord their God. God Himself will go before him, in the spirit of Elijah, to turn the hearts of fathers to their children and the rebellious to the wisdom of the just, and to prepare for the Lord a people well-disposed."[9]

---

[9]Luke 1:13-17

Mary thought: "*to prepare for the Lord...*" The Angel was talking about her Son, the Child in her womb; *He* was the Lord! How would all these things happen? How would this child in her arms, Elizabeth's baby, be great in the Eyes of the Lord? How would he bring back the sons of Israel? How would he prepare the way for the Lord?

We're told that Mary pondered many things in her heart, after Jesus was found in the Temple.[10] But when did it begin? Was it after Jesus was lost and then found, or did it begin even before His birth? As she looked down at the infant John in her arms, he who would precede her Son, did she contemplate what life would be like for them?

Do we relate to Mary in this Mystery? Do we have the freedom to turn everything over to Jesus, and thank Him for the joys and the sorrows? Remember, while Mary was praising God for her singular honor, in the back of her mind, she knew there would be sadness mixed with the bliss. Every action has a reaction. Every positive has had a negative, and every negative a positive. God balances it all out.

Sing your own Magnificat! Raise your arms and your heart to God in Thanksgiving for all the gifts He has ever given you, those of joy, as well as those of sorrow. Don't just accept the bad with the good; embrace it! God is in charge. He makes all things work.

✝

Oh, Lord we pray that we, like John the Baptist, may recognize You in our lives. And in so doing, we, too, may leap for joy. From the time, the Holy Spirit entered Elizabeth's womb and John became filled with Him, he had the Signal Grace to live for Jesus and to die for Him. Oh Lord, we know that we are in the time of John the Baptist. Give us the courage and the grace to pave the way for Your Second Coming!

---

[10]Luke 2:51

The Birth of Our Lord Jesus

The excitement builds, as we approach the birth of the Savior. Three kings have left their countries, following the bright star in the east. In far-off Rome, Caesar Augustus is issuing a decree: The entire Roman Empire must be counted. Each person had to return to his birthplace.

And then, there is Joseph and Mary. Under normal conditions, this would not seem like a great burden to go from Nazareth to Bethlehem, less than a week's journey by foot. But these were not normal times. How could he possibly subject Mary to such a trip, now? She was heavy with Child. She should not be traveling anywhere, no less on rough roads, over high mountains. She was extremely healthy, but she was entering her *ninth month*! Did these fears run through Joseph's mind, as he read the notice posted on the door of the synagogue?

When Joseph shared this news with Mary, what was her reaction? We believe, her heart jumped for joy. Was it not another *powerful* affirmation that she was carrying the Son of God? She knew well the Scripture passages: The Messiah would be born in Bethlehem. Had she wondered how the Lord was going to arrange that?

Was this her answer? She must have been so excited. It was beginning! You can bet, Joseph's and Mary's attitudes were at opposite ends of the spectrum. He was most likely worried about many things; she probably wanted to get on the road. He didn't know where they would stay, how Mary would manage the trip; she knew God would provide. She was carrying *His Son* inside her. She had to know that Legions of Angels would surround and protect them and the precious unborn Babe, as they traveled to Bethlehem, that Gabriel would be covering Mary with his wings, protecting her from the elements, while Michael was clearing the road of anyone who might threaten their safe passage.

†

Bethlehem is the city of David. Joseph was from the lineage of David. He came from Bethlehem. He had many relatives there; but he hadn't visited them in some time. Add to that, everyone else who was born in Bethlehem was returning to be counted in the census. When Joseph and Mary arrived in Bethlehem, it was even worse than he had suspected. The town was jammed with people. He tried the inns first; there was no room. He tried his relatives; most didn't even remember him; and those who did, had no room. It was impossible. Desperate, he went back to the inns, again. He was willing to pay whatever they wanted, even though he was not a rich man. No amount of money would do it. No one had a room for them. Now, after the fact, we *all* would die to welcome Jesus, Mary and Joseph into our homes, offering them the finest room in our home. But no one knew them, and they were not welcome anywhere.

Joseph found a cave on the outskirts of town, whose only other tenant was an ox. Joseph led Mary inside. He carefully arranged hay for her to lie down on. She was exhausted from the journey, but she was calm and joyful; nothing ruffled her; she was anticipating what she knew was to come at any time. Joseph felt the same way, but he manifested his exhilaration by taking charge, and *doing things*. He asked Mary to try to sleep. He went over to the opening of the cave to keep guard.

It is true that no one knows exactly what happened that night that God came to the face of the earth. But, please forgive us if we dream. Mary felt the Lord calling her. She got up, and looked up into the sky. The moon was so bright! The curtains of Heaven parted. Angels poured out, gently making their way down to earth, taking their positions for the great event which was about to take place. The gaze of the Holy Spirit beamed down on her, enveloping her, in the form of a brilliant light. The light was so intense, it seemed as if it were feeding life into her. Her entire body trembled from the power that was encompassing her. Her heart beat so vigorously, she thought it would jump out of her body. It was happening! It was now! She felt a great burning of love in her heart for God.[1] It was done. He was here!

Gloria in Excelsis Deo!

The sound of Angels chanting, praising God for the gift, He was giving the world at this moment, reverberated throughout the valley, ricocheting off the hills and mountains, shaking the very earth with its power. The vibration of the Angels' voices and the excited fluttering of their wings wakened shepherds, sleeping in the nearby fields. They rushed out of their caves to see what the commotion was. There, before them, was a Legion of Angels!

In another place, a distance away, the eyes of the three kings darted sharply in the direction of the tremor that shook them out of a deep sleep. They had been following the bright star. It stopped moving over Bethlehem. *Now they knew the direction to follow.*

Back in Jerusalem, Herod angrily *ripped* open the curtains of his palace. He glared out at the bright sky, suspiciously studying each gleaming star. He had been rudely awakened from his deep sleep. He had felt a terrifying rumble, like the very earth trembling beneath his feet. He didn't know what it was, but he didn't like it.

Did You cry, Jesus as You entered the world? The gentle sound of the Baby reached out to Joseph. He looked around the room, aware for the first time of the brilliant light within. The first thing he saw was Mary's face. She was

---

[1]St. Teresa of Avila used this expression to describe the transverberation of her heart. More on St. Teresa in Bob and Penny's book: *"Saints and other Powerful Women in the Church"*.

radiant. Tears were streaming down her beautiful cheeks. Her eyes were looking beyond him, to the heavens above, focused on the source of the light streaming in. Joseph followed the light to Mary's arms. She held the softest, whitest, most delicate Child, Joseph had ever seen. The King, the Messiah, was born! *The Word was made Flesh!*

At first, Joseph didn't know what to do. How do you behave in the presence of God? He was awkward. But the gentle Mary, who had turned from girl into woman in nine short months, encouraged him with her eyes, and motioned for him to come closer. It was awesome! He would be responsible for this Child's welfare for many years. It was time to begin. The Holy couple wrapped the Baby in swaddling clothes.[2] They arranged Him comfortably on a bed of hay. Mary lay close to Him, with Joseph kneeling at her side. The light dimmed. The Angels stationed themselves around the cave, keeping *out* those who should not enter, and allowing *in* those whom the Lord wanted in.

Joseph and Mary were exhausted from the excitement of the evening. They had just begun to doze, when they heard feet shuffling outside the cave. Joseph shot up. To his amazement, he saw simple shepherds standing outside the cave, peering within. They entered the cave slowly, a look of both fear and anticipation on their faces. They recounted how *Angels* had been in the fields, singing praises to God, and how they told them to come to this cave, where they would see the *King of the World.*

Joseph was speechless; he couldn't fully take in all that was happening before his very eyes. Mary raised herself, so that the shepherds could get a better look at the Child in her

---

[2]Luke 2:7 *"wrapped Him in swaddling clothes."* It has been said that Mary weaved the swaddling garment without a seam. This was strictly reserved for those of royal birth, affirming our Lord's Kingship. There is a legend that Jesus' *burial* cloth was the same one that was wrapped around Him when He was born.

arms. They knelt and paid homage to Him. Joseph and Mary listened, as the shepherds told them that the Angel said: *"You have nothing to fear! I come to proclaim good news to you - tidings of great joy to be shared by the whole people. This day in David's city a Savior has been born to you, the Messiah and Lord. Let this be a sign to you: in a manger you will find an Infant wrapped in swaddling clothes."*[3]

Mary searched their faces. There was such joy and hope in their eyes. She recalled the Angel's words *to her: "He will be great, and He will be called Son of the Most High. The Lord God will give Him the throne of His ancestor David; he will rule over the house of Jacob forever, and His kingdom will have no end."*

Now as the world was about to receive her King, in Jerusalem a king of the world was plotting to kill that King. Three kings from the East had stopped at the palace of King Herod inquiring: *"'Where is the King of the Jews? We observed His star rising and have come to pay Him homage.' At this news King Herod became greatly disturbed, and with him all Jerusalem."*[4] Herod asked his chief priest and scribes where this King was to be born. When they told him, the Messiah was to be born in Bethlehem, he bid the kings go there, and report back to him, so that he could go and pay Him homage. The three kings set out toward Bethlehem. They followed the star they had first seen, to this place.

Now, they peered inside, awe-struck by the Heavenly Sight before them - the Infant Child with His Mother Mary. They knelt and paid homage to Jesus. Then they presented the Babe *"with gifts of gold, frankincense, and myrrh."*[5] When they were warned in a dream to not return to Herod, they

---

[3]Luke 2:10-12

[4]Matt 2:2-3

[5]Matt 2:11 Gifts of gold, frankincense and myrrh were customary in the East as signs of homage paid.

took a different route back to their country, bypassing Jerusalem altogether.

Mary kept a mental record of these events all the days of her life. A time would come when she would need to draw on these memories for strength.

†

As you share this Mystery, set your heart on the *true* gift of Christmas, the gift of *Jesus*. The enemy tries his hardest, each year, to cloud the *real* issue of Christmas, the birth of the Savior. He tries to mask it with tinsel and artificial snow and stockings hung from the chimney with care. He tries to make the hero of Christmas, Frosty the Snowman, or Rudolph the Red-nosed Reindeer, or even Santa Claus. Santa Claus, or more properly *Saint Nicholas*, would be the first to tell you that the gift he brings you on Christmas, the only gift that counts, is the helpless little Baby Who was born to die for the salvation of the world.

Our minds and hearts go back to Mount Tabor in the Holy Land. Four mosaics surround the main Altar. The one that touched us deeply was that of the Baby Jesus. The Angels were hovering over Him, their eyes heavenward, glorifying their Lord. You are so filled with joy and rejoicing; then your eyes travel to the Babe in the manger below the Angels. He is so beautiful, so precious as you look at His Baby Cheeks. You want to reach out and fondly hold those chubby Cheeks in your hands, close to your face. But suddenly, your joy turns to sorrow; you feel like crying. His Eyes! My God, His Eyes are like those of an old Man, like those of Someone Who has seen all the sorrows of the world; and those sorrows are in These Eyes. When you look in the Eyes of this Babe, you can see why our Lord was born. Did you see any of this in your newborn Son, Mother Mary?

One year, our Junior Legion of Mary[6] put on an Easter play. The children played all the parts, including Jesus. On Good Friday, our Pastor Monsignor O'Connell used the play as a meditation on the seven last words of Jesus. I think the most poignant time in the play was when the lights dimly came up on a young boy (our grandson - ten years old at the time), bleeding on the Cross, and in the corner a scene of Joseph and Mary with the Baby Jesus in her arms. We have never forgotten that moment in our lives. When Jesus asked us to give up everything and follow Him, we remembered that scene, and *we said yes*!

One of the happiest Christmas seasons I can remember in my life was, when I was eleven or twelve. I decided to go to the 6 a.m. Mass every morning from the beginning of Advent to Christmas day. I don't know why I did it. At the time, I thought that the Lord wanted me to give *Him* that gift; but the gift was for me. Through rain and snow and bitter-cold weather, I went to a little Dominican Monastery about four blocks from my home, every day from Thanksgiving to Christmas. Many years have passed; I can still smell the candles burning in that Chapel; I can still hear the nuns singing their morning prayers. That time, that gift, will be with me for the rest of my life. My memories bring it out, dust it off, and play it for me every Advent season.

Meditate with Mother Mary on the *Miracle of Christmas*, on the Incarnation, the Word made Flesh, God among us. Relive the *true* story of Christmas in your mind and heart, in your home, with your family. Go to Mass every morning. Give that gift to the Baby Jesus. See what He gives you in return. Get ready for the Savior to be born in your heart, as you receive Him in Holy Communion. Are you ready? Here He comes!

---

[6]Bob and Penny write about this in: *"We came back to Jesus"*

The Presentation

Eight days have passed since that very special moment when the world stood still and Our Savior was born. We see Joseph and Mary bringing the Infant Jesus to the Temple in Jerusalem, in keeping with the Mosaic laws. They were following the tradition of their people, in obedience to the tenets of their Faith: *"Every first-born male must be consecrated to the Lord."*[1] They *knew* this Child was the Son of God and above the ordinances that man must follow; but never, for one moment, did they think this precluded them from obeying the law of their ancestors. Therefore, they made the journey from Bethlehem to Jerusalem. They weren't prepared for what was to happen to them there.

We don't know if Joseph or Mary ever considered *how* the world would learn about Jesus. They knew what the Angel had revealed to each of them, as well as to Zechariah and Elizabeth. But this was all within the confines of their family. They believed in the specialness of their Son, Who had been conceived by the the Holy Spirit; but they didn't know *how* the Father would manifest His Son's presence and mission to the rest of the world. *Well, they were about to find out, pretty quickly.*

---

[1]Luke 2:23-24

Mary and Joseph did everything that was required under the law of Moses. On this day of Circumcision, it was customary to bring a *spotless lamb* and a turtledove for sacrifice. But as they were too poor, Joseph could only bring a pair of turtledoves. Didn't he realize that he had brought the Spotless Lamb, the Son Whom God had entrusted to him. Joseph and Mary's hearts beat excitedly, as they climbed to the entrance of the Temple.

There was a lot of activity going on, people going in and out of the Temple. To their amazement, it seemed as if someone was frantically calling out to them. They whirled around to see where it was coming from. There was no one there, except for an old man sitting on the steps, his head bowed low. It couldn't have been him, they thought. He raised his head and stared at them. They entered the Temple; the old man followed them. He was still making sounds, but now they were more like moans of joy mixed with pain. His eyes were riveted on the Baby. Mary laid Jesus on the table, in preparation for His Circumcision. The old man seemed harmless enough to Joseph and Mary, but she became startled when he took the Baby in his arms.

The old man raised his head towards Heaven, and praised the Lord.

> *"Now, Master, You can dismiss Your servant in peace;*
> *You have fulfilled your word.*
> *For my eyes have witnessed your saving deed displayed for all the peoples to see:*
> *A revealing light to the Gentiles,*
> *the glory of Your people Israel."*[2]

Scripture tells us **"The Child's father and mother were marveling at what was being said about Him."**[3] At first blush, we have to wonder why Joseph and Mary were

---

[2]Luke 2:29-32
[3]Luke 2:33-34

marveling. Had not the Angel told them that Mary would give birth to the Son of God? Was it that they did not expect it to be revealed so soon? Simeon recognized Jesus as the Messiah, the moment he saw Him. He prophesied Jesus' mission, immediately. How did he know this? Luke tells us the Holy Spirit entered into the old man.[4]

Now, stand beside Mary as she looks at Simeon. He turns from the Baby to her, and prophesies:

"This child is destined to be the downfall and the rise of many in Israel, a sign that will be opposed - and you yourself shall be pierced with a sword - so that the thoughts of many hearts may be laid bare."[5]

Did she watch his eyes as he spoke? With his first words, her heart had leapt with joy. The Angel Gabriel's words to her were confirmed! My God, what was he saying, now? She understood *"the rise of many"*, but what did he mean: *"the downfall of many in Israel"*? How could this be? Her Son was to be the *Savior* of Israel. He was to free His People from slavery. How could Simeon have given her a gift that lifted her spirit to the heights of joy only to wound her with words that had to plunge her into the deepest sorrow? What was this man saying? What did this prophecy mean to her Son? Those whose *downfall* he would bring about, would they hurt Him? Did you suddenly feel a pain in your heart, Mary? Did a sword pierce your heart?

Mary was a young girl. She wasn't supposed to be able to understand what Simeon was saying. He was speaking words far beyond her age, words of wisdom from a sage, a prophet. How was she supposed to understand what they meant? Yet, she clung to them. She listened intently, not necessarily understanding completely what was being said,

---

[4]Luke 2:25-27
[5]Luke 2:34-35

but knowing and accepting that her road would be a hard one. Mary *said yes* one more time!

No sooner had Simeon finished than another old person, this time a woman, entered the room. It was Anna, the prophetess. A widow for many years, she spent just about all her time in the Temple. As soon as Anna saw the Baby, she knew she was in the presence of the Almighty. She began to praise God, and tell anyone who would listen that this Child would be responsible for the *deliverance* of Jerusalem. Did Mary think: *That's more like it*!?

Mary listened intently to the words of the woman. Mary liked Anna. It was obvious, Anna was taken with the Baby Jesus. Her eyes shone with love, as she knelt before Him. It had to be the Holy Spirit who had revealed all that had been said by the two prophets; they had not had a chance to speak and arrange their words ahead of time. There was no logical explanation why these two, a prophet and a prophetess, would know so much about her Baby.

All the things that had happened to Mary in the past year came back to her. The words of the Angel Gabriel, when he appeared to her in Nazareth, were all coming to pass. It seemed so long ago, that time in Nazareth, and yet it was only nine months ago. So much had happened in her life since then. She had been a child then, a special child, but a child, nonetheless. Now she was a mother, a protective mother, a concerned mother, a strong mother if need be, but unquestionably a mother.

These people were talking about her Child! True, He was the Son of God, but He was also her *Child*. He was Flesh of her flesh; her blood flowed through Him. She had known Him in a way that no one had or would ever know Him. He had grown inside her. She heard His first Heart Beat. She felt the first time He kicked his tiny Foot within her womb. She knew Him from the moment He was conceived by the Holy Spirit. Now, she would accept the responsibility, she had been entrusted with; to care for Him, to guard Him from all danger, to nourish Him not only with physical food but spiritual food of Holy Scripture. She had listened carefully for anything that might be threatening to her Baby. She would not forget any of their words.

What these two people did was affirm her mission. The three wise men, kings themselves, had bowed to her Son respecting Him as a King above all other kings. Now, the reality of what they had said and done was coming to Mother Mary. Her role as *Mother of the Messiah* was being proclaimed in the Temple! For the first time since her Baby was born, she had to take her place as *Queen Mother*. All well and good; but for now, she would be His protectress. Mary the Mother snugly wrapped her Baby in cloth; she lifted Him from the table; and holding Him close, she signaled Joseph it was time to leave.

This is not the place where Luke tells us Mary stored all these things in her heart. But we have to believe it was *one* of those times, and an important one at that. Her future role in history became well-defined at this time. She became like a tigress where her Child was concerned, caring for Him, and shielding Him until that day she no longer could.

†

In the Cathedral of Notre Dame in Paris, there is a statue of Our Lady of Paris, holding the Infant Jesus. She is very regal, truly a Queen. She actually welcomes you to the Cathedral. But, she guards her Child, her elbow thrust out, protecting Him; there is a look on her face that warns you not to take a chance on attempting to harm Him in any way, or you will have to deal with her. During the French Revolution, the Cathedral was abused terribly. At one point, it was used as a barn and storage area. Lewd dances were performed around the main altar by nude women. We have to believe that Our Lady of Paris was not happy with the treatment her Son was receiving at that time. There was probably even a tear or two which trickled down the cheek of that statue. She had to stand by and see Him hurt, one more time.

But a few years ago, the 200th anniversary of the Revolution was held in France. All the people who desecrated Mary and her Son Jesus are gone, to worship for time *in memoriam* the false god they chose on earth. These authors of violence and merciless carnage became *victims* of the Reign of Terror they created. But Mary is still there in that Cathedral. So is Jesus. And while we get really upset at the atrocities committed against Our Lord Jesus and His Mother Mary, and rightfully so, keep in mind that Jesus and Mother Mary are still here, and will continue to be here. God is in charge; God is always in charge. Don't cry for Them; cry for ourselves and our children.

This is a joyful mystery, true, but it's a joyful mystery mixed with sadness. In light of the prophecy of Simeon to Mary, she *had* to know that she would realize the joy of being present when Israel would be freed from the bonds of tyranny; but the shadow, cast on this ray of sunshine, was the gnawing inside her of what the cost might possibly be. [There is a tradition in our Church that the little Boy Jesus had a nightmare in which He saw an Angel carrying a Cross and another Angel holding nails (the means that would be used to nail our precious Lord to the Cross). He ran to His Mother. In the painting of *Our Lady of Perpetual Help*, we see Jesus, the little Person clinging to His Mother, one of His shoes having fallen off, in His haste to the safety of His Mother's arms.]

†

We believe, the gift Mary was given at this time, in addition to affirmation of her role, and her Son's role in the world, was *determination*, the decision to do whatever it takes. Through Simeon, the Lord allowed her to see a very small part of what she would have to say *Yes* to, what she would have to endure. Perhaps it began here, with the prophecy. Was this the first sword to pierce her heart? Did Simeon prophesy only seven swords, or did we just count up the most *piercing* thrusts which ripped into her heart?

We have walked with Joseph and Mary to Jerusalem, as in *obedience* to the Law, they presented Jesus to the Lord. *"Consecrate to Me every first-born that opens the womb among the Israelites....It belongs to Me."*[6] When Mary said Yes to this consecration of her Son to God the Father, she began *her* walk to the Cross. We will share the many times that Mary is given the message that her Son will suffer. As she gives every *Yes*, our Lord walks one step closer to His Passion and death on the Cross, and she with Him. The prophet Simeon told Mary that the Messiah, the Anointed One, would be the *"consolation of Israel"*. Who will be your consolation, Mother Mary as you stand beneath the Cross?

Her great Fiat, her *Yes* to the Angel Gabriel was just the *beginning*, the first in a lifetime of *Yeses*, most of which would have been enough for any mother to scream from the pit of her stomach, *"Stop! Enough! I can't do it!"* But Mary kept going, determined to do whatever it took to fulfill the Lord's Will. We do not know, if at the very beginning, she had been given a look at all she would be called to suffer, she would have been able to handle it. But the Lord never gives us more than we can carry. One day at a time, that's all He asks for, only today. Yesterday is gone; there is nothing we can do about it. Tomorrow has troubles of its own. Live for today. Say *Yes* today, and watch how it washes clean yesterday, and changes tomorrow into a beautiful today. Do as Mary did. Give Our Lord Jesus your ongoing *Yes*. Start today, now!

---

[6]Ex 3:2

The Finding of Jesus in the Temple

In the final Joyful Mystery, we see the bridge that Jesus and Mary will cross to the Sorrowful Mysteries and the Passion. We become aware that the path, Jesus has begun to take, will lead Him to Calvary. Up till now, His Mission on earth has been revealed by others. Gabriel calls Jesus the *Son of God*.[1] Then, Simeon[2] and Anna[3] prophesy Jesus' ministry. Now, it is time for Jesus to reveal to the world Who He is and Who His Father is. Again, Mary will feel her heart pierced with a sword.

On the surface, it would seem that all that is happening in The Fifth Joyful mystery is that Jesus is lost and then three days later, He is found preaching in the Temple. In this mystery, if we are not careful, we dwell on that and not its link with the Incarnation, and the Passion. Jesus told Pilate: "*The reason I was born, the reason I came into the world, is to testify to the truth.*"[4] Jesus is announcing the reason He was born, why God became Man. In the Fifth Mystery, Jesus says to His Mother: "*Did you not know I had to be about My Father's work?*"[5] We see, here, the Boy Jesus; but He is speaking as a Man Who knows His Mission and is saying Yes, pleading with His Mother to do the same. We start to get a glimpse of the Jesus Who will say to His Father, as He suffers the agony in the Garden:

> "*Father, if it is possible, let this chalice pass from Me. Nevertheless, not as I will, but as Thou wilt.*"[6]

---

[1]Luke 1:35
[2]Luke 1:29-32
[3]Luke 1:38
[4]John 18:37
[5]Luke 2:49-50
[6]Matt 26:39

Each year, the Holy Family went to Jerusalem for the Passover, in accordance with the Law. A whole group from the town would go together in caravan, for safety reasons. Pilgrimages were very dangerous, what with robbers ready to waylay pilgrims on their way to Jerusalem. They would also travel together for company.

Men traveled in one part of the caravan, while the women traveled with the children in another. Prior to this year, there had never been a confusion; Jesus traveled with Mary. But then, He was a Child. However this, Jesus' twelfth year, we find Him traveling with Joseph. Did Our Lady want Him to come with her, this one last time? Did Joseph playfully chide her: "*You have to let go a little, Mother. The Child is becoming of age.*"

Mary had always known Who her Son Jesus was. She had never forgotten the visit of the Angel, her conceiving by the Holy Spirit, her visit with her cousin Elizabeth, the events surrounding Jesus' birth: the shepherds, the Angels, the kings from the east, the messages to Joseph in a dream, the prophecies of Simeon and Anna. All these events were vividly imprinted on her heart. She could never forget them.

So when, at the end of the first day's journey back to Nazareth, she discovered that her Son, the Son of God, the Savior of the world, her Charge, was not with her or her husband, panic set in. Her mind raced, as she and Joseph rushed back to Jerusalem. She thought about the words of the Angel: "*Great will be His dignity, and He will be called Son of the Most High.*"[7] She had been given responsibility for this Boy, this Son of God the Most High, and she had lost Him. **Is it too far-fetched to believe she prayed**: "*Dear Lord, if you let us find Him, if you give me this one more chance, I vow, I will never let anything happen to Him again. I promise that with my life. No one or nothing will influence me.*"? Oh, Mary

---

[7]Luke 1:32

how many times we make vows we cannot keep. We will walk with you through this agony, when you do not know where your Son is, and what is happening to Him. Was the Father preparing you for that next time, Calvary?

What was St. Joseph's pain, as he recalled the many times he had protected this precious Child with Whom he had been entrusted? Oh, how very much he loved Him! He had grown too quickly; the time had flown. It seems that one day, he is being told by the Angel to flee into Egypt because the Baby Jesus is in danger,[8] and the next he is searching for the Boy Who is lost. Like so many of us parents, Joseph was frightened, he would never again see this Child he loved so very dearly. Those who have adopted children will tell you that you love these children every bit as much as if they were born of your flesh and blood.

When a child is lost, the parent goes through the years, moment by moment: What should I have done differently? How could I have let this happen? St. Joseph had kept the Boy Jesus close to him, teaching Him the honorable craft of carpenter. He had watched Him grow from a little Baby making curls out of wood-shavings to an apprentice. Oh, the joy of sharing each moment of this special Boy's life! Had he taken Him for granted, and now He was lost? If there is a Purgatory on earth, this must have been one for St. Joseph.

St. Joseph, did you and Mary talk? Did you share your pain with her? Did you pray to the Father to wake you from this nightmare? How excitedly the three of you had looked forward to this pilgrimage to Jerusalem. How proud you were of your Charge, as you brought him to the Temple. And now He was nowhere to be found.

We don't know how long it took Mary and Joseph to find Jesus. We don't know where all they looked. It's easy to be wise in retrospect. We say today, "*Well, of course, they*

---

[8]Matt 2:13

looked in the Temple. That's natural." But we don't know that. They probably looked all over town. They might have even gone to the police, before going to the Temple. They were most likely backtracking, retracing all their steps, going back to all the places they had been. Going back to the Temple may have been a last ditch effort.

We can only try to imagine Mary's emotional state, as she walked into the Temple area with Joseph, completely distraught, to see her Son, sitting calmly among the elders of the Temple, asking and answering questions. Mary's humanity is very much like ours, at this point. She had to be relieved, but that was *soon* followed by hurt! Mother Mary was hurt! How could He do this to them? They had always been such a close family. He had never done anything like this before? Did He realize how serious this was? She cried out: "*Son, why have you done this to us? You see that your father and I have been searching for you in sorrow.*"[9] Another sword pierced her heart - *sorrow*. Were her thoughts: *Oh, Son if I should have lost you forever, I don't think I could stand it*?

She was not prepared for His answer: "*Why did you search for me? Did you not know I had to be in My Father's House?*"[10] I am sure Jesus did not want to cause His Mother and foster father any pain. But, if you remember He will later say: "*Whoever loves father and mother more than Me, is not worthy of Me.*"[11] Not even His love for Mother Mary and St. Joseph could stand in the way of His doing the Father's Will. Our Lord is a God of mercy, and the most merciful thing He could do for His Mother is to now start to pave the way, the Way of the Cross. He had to begin to prepare her, for His time was about to begin; the next eighteen years would fly! With His words, was Jesus not really saying that

---

[9]Luke 2:48
[10]Luke 2:49-50
[11]Matt 10:47

this was the reason He was here, the reason He came to earth in the first place? With these words, was He not saying, in effect, *"You, more than any other should understand what I am doing. This is what it's all about."*

After the initial fright wore off, Mary must have marveled at what her Son was *doing*, teaching the teachers. Jesus, her twelve year old was preaching in the Temple![12] Where else should He be? She knew, but she may not have wanted to know. Did she try to tell herself, *"If I don't think about it, maybe it won't happen. If I put it out of my mind, it will forestall the inevitable. I know what He is called to do in this world. Father, please give us some more time."* Were the Angel's words coming to life? *"The Lord God will give Him the throne of David His father. He will rule over the house of Jacob forever, and His reign will be without end."*[13] Did the words of the prophet Simeon, *"You yourself shall be pierced with a sword - so that the thoughts of many hearts may be laid bare."*[14] come to her? Did she cry out in the silence of her heart to the Lord she so loved, *"Not yet, Lord. It's too soon!"*

When she first saw her Son, she had cried out: *"Son, why have you done this to us? You see that your father and I have been searching for You in sorrow."*

What was she supposed to answer *when He said: "Why did you search for me? Did you not know I had to be in my Father's House?"*

Should she have said: *"Oh, that's right, Son. I'm sorry. I didn't realize it would begin so soon. I thought we'd have more time together as a family, but now I understand."* Well, she couldn't, just yet. And she knew He would understand.

---

[12]In the Jewish Faith, a boy prepares for his Bar Mitzvah, and when he reaches 13 years old, he addresses the elders of the Temple. It is said, the fact that Jesus was in the Temple addressing the elders at 12 years old verifies the fact that He had no *earthly* father.

[13]Luke 1:32

[14]Luke 2:35

Was God preparing her for the time when she would be separated from Him, and have to remain on earth without Him for seventeen years,[15] what had to seem like seventeen lifetimes?

†

We read that Jesus was lost in Jerusalem; then three days later, He was found in the temple. What it doesn't tell us is that this is actually the first recorded event in Scripture where Jesus preaches. It was in fact, the beginning of His public life. Scripture doesn't tell us very much about Jesus during His growing years, prior to this event. All we have is a mention in Luke's Gospel, *"The Child grew and became strong; He was full of wisdom, and God's blessings were upon Him."*[16] And yet the very next passage, we see Jesus talking to the elders in the temple in Jerusalem. Think about it. We're talking about a twelve year old, keeping the elders entranced with His knowledge and wisdom. Orthodox Jewish men spend their whole lives interpreting and reinterpreting Holy Scripture, and here was a mere Boy opening their minds to the Torah, the Word of God, with wisdom beyond any of their oldest scholars.

We see two strong characters in this Mystery on the life of Our Lord: Jesus as a Youth, and His Mother Mary.

"Son, why have you done this to us?" are Mary's first recorded words to Jesus in the Bible. *"Why did you search for me?"* are *Jesus'* first recorded words to Mary in the Bible. Where did St. Luke, the Evangelist, get these words? We know the Gospel is inspired, but still, none of the other Evangelists had been given this kind of insight into the intimate moments of Jesus, Mary and the Holy Family.

We believe that Luke was given the precious gift of knowing Our Lady in a very special way. We can just picture

---

[15]according to Sister Mary Agreda in *City of God*
[16]Luke 3:40

him sitting at her feet, listening for hours to her, as she recounted the early years of Jesus, their experiences, the adventures of the Holy Family. Twice in the same chapter, Luke makes reference to Our Lady's "*holding these things in her heart.*" In the account of the shepherds coming to the manger, he says, "*Mary treasured all these things and reflected on them in her heart.*"[17] Then again, in the account of the Finding of Jesus in the Temple, Luke says, "*His mother meanwhile kept all these things in her memory.*"[18]

There are so many things said, in the unsaid. If only we would open our hearts to listen. There is so much to learn through the relationship between Mary and her Divine Son; but especially during those years, during this one incident which was the beginning of Jesus out in the world, and the beginning of the end.

Mary kept all these things in her heart. How many things did she keep in her heart; how many times did the Lord remind her why she was given the gift of being His Mother, and why He had come into the world? How often did she have to be reminded, so that she would never talk herself into thinking theirs could be a normal life? He was special; she was special. There was a price for that specialness. He was born to die. She was born to share in His suffering and death. His whole life was in preparation for being the instrument of our redemption on the Cross. She was born to witness it, to stand by Him, to hold back the tears as she told Him "*It's all right, Son. You can carry that Cross. I'll walk with You. I'll be right there by Your side. I say yes. Let it be done unto me according to Your will.*"

†

Oh, Lord that we might be found preaching in Your Temple when You come, again.

---

[17]Luke 2:19
[18]Luke 2:51

The Agony in the Garden

Our Lord Jesus loves us so much, He made detailed preparations for our well-being, right up to the end of His life. He wanted to have a *last* supper with His disciples. He had instructions for them. He wanted to be sure they understood their role in Salvation History, and how they were to conduct themselves. He wanted to leave them and His Church ammunition for the days ahead.

He washed their feet. Peter protested. Jesus told him, *"Unless I wash your feet, you cannot share in My heritage."*[1]

Then Jesus explained why He had washed their feet.

"What I just did was to give you an example: as I have done, so you must do. I solemnly assure you, no slave is greater than his master; no messenger outranks the one who sent him. Once you know all these things, blest will you be if you put them into practice."[2]

In case they had joined Him because of the glory, was Jesus reminding them that the glory is always bought by *pain, persecution*, and *anguish*? We recall His answer when the mother of James and John asked if her sons would be seated in Heaven, one at His right and one at His left: He asked

---

[1]John 13:8
[2]John 13:15-17

75

James and John if they were ready to drink from the cup from which He would drink. Little did they know the cup Jesus was talking about, when they said yes! Jesus took that yes and later sent His Holy Spirit down to give them the strength to fulfill that promise.

Was He trying to teach them, with this act of washing their feet: that if they wanted the rewards, they had to be ready to pay the price? Could they imitate Him in big and *little* things? Could they learn *how* to be humble from Him?

He gave them the gift of His Body and Blood in the Eucharist. He fulfilled the promise He made, "*I will be with you always, until the end of the world.*"[3] They didn't understand it at the time, but after the Holy Spirit entered into them, they realized the Gift He was leaving them.

One of our early Church Fathers said that the Church would not have lasted one hundred years without the Eucharist. Jesus had overheard them squabbling over who would be first. He had seen how they had wanted to stay on Mount Tabor after witnessing His *glorious* Transfiguration. He knew that His three trusted Apostles would not have the strength to stay awake one hour with Him in the Garden of Gethsemane. How would these eleven be able to live and die for His Church? (He knew the twelfth would betray Him.) He knew those He had chosen were not the wisest, bravest, strongest of men. How would they and His Church survive? He would give them, and the Bishops and priests who would follow, the grace and power to overcome all adversaries, even unto death for the Faith. He left Himself: His Body, Blood, Soul and Divinity in the Holy Eucharist.

He tried to prepare them for the rough days ahead.

Although His strong focus this evening, was that of putting all things in order for His disciples, and His Church, the upcoming events kept breaking through His

---

[3]Matt 28:20

consciousness. He couldn't help but think about them. Jesus knew they had not fully realized why He had come to earth. He knew the pain and disappointment, the fear they would experience when they saw the Son of God die on the Cross. His thoughts were of them when He said, "*What I say is not said of all, for I know the kind of men I choose.*" [He was trying to reassure and affirm those who were not betraying Him.] "*My purpose here is the fulfillment of Scripture. He who partook of bread with Me has raised his heel against Me.*" Then He said, "*One of you will betray Me.*"[4] He watched as all questioned each other, and then asked Him: "*Is it I, Lord?*"[5] Finally, when Judas asked the question, Jesus pinned him down, "*It is you who have said it.*" Then He gave Judas his instructions, "*Be quick about what you are to do.*"[6] after which Judas left.

Jesus gave them a last teaching. He predicted they would *all* leave Him. When Peter exclaimed he would never leave Him, Jesus predicted that before the cock crowed twice, Peter would deny Him three times. But it was said with *love!* Jesus knew their weaknesses. [There is a tradition that Peter cried so much because he had denied his Lord three times that there were ruts coming down his face from the tears.] Jesus knew, it would take the power of the Holy Spirit to give the Apostles the courage they needed, to carry out the mandate He had given them. He prayed over them. Then they left for the Garden of Gethsemane.

Jesus sang! This is the only time in Scripture we hear of Jesus singing.[7] [St. Augustine tells us that when we sing (well) we pray twice.] Jesus knew, He and they would have to have *strength* to live through the days ahead. Previously, He had brought Peter, James and John to the top of a

---

[4]Matt 26:23
[5]Matt 26:22
[6]Matt 26:25
[7]Matt 26:30

mountain, Mount Tabor and strengthened them by showing them His transfigured Self. They had been so overjoyed, they wanted to stay up there forever. What they did not know; this was to lead to another high place - Calvary.

All of them sang as they left the Upper Room; and they continued singing as they walked past Caiphas' palace, where Jesus would return that very night under much different circumstances. They crossed over the Kidron Valley on to the Garden of Gethsemane, at the foot of the Mount of Olives. This was a favorite place of Jesus. It was near Bethany, the home of Lazarus, Martha and Mary. This area was where Jesus stayed whenever He came into Jerusalem. He never stayed in the city, but outside, on this side. It was on the Mount of Olives that he wept over Jerusalem and predicted its destruction, which took place some thirty seven years after His death and Resurrection. It was here that He said:

"Jerusalem, Jerusalem, you who kill the prophets and stone those sent to you, how many times I yearned to gather your children together, as a hen gathers her young under her wings, but you were unwilling! Behold your house will be abandoned, desolate. I tell you, you will not see Me again until you say, 'Blessed is He who comes in the name of the Lord.'"[8]

Jesus took Peter, James and John with Him into the Garden. He asked them to stand guard and pray. Then Jesus went off by Himself, to pray at the rock. Jesus knew *why* He had been sent to the earth. This was the beginning of the end of His Mission, the salvation of men and their sins. We believe that Jesus was able to see, in that short time, all the sins that had ever been committed by man and would be committed until the end of time. He grieved over the blatant betrayal against His Father by man, down through the centuries.

---

[8]Matt 23:37

We know He must have seen the brutal outrage against humanity, committed by Mao Tse-Tung, Josef Stalin and Adolf Hitler in this twentieth century. He must have cried as He witnessed the carnage, the mass genocide of close to *forty million* of His children by these monsters. How this must have pierced His Side, and strangled His heart. He also had to see the more than *thirty million* victims of abortion at the hands of their own mothers, the new monsters, in our country alone. And this is not counting the staggering number of victims, in other so-called *civilized* countries throughout the world, who are falling for Satan's plan for annihilation of the world. Jesus had to realize that the worst atrocities against humanity were to be committed after His great sacrifice, and the triumph of the Cross. Is this when He began to bleed? Did knowledge of all the sins of the world, before and after Him, cause such pressure on His Head and Heart, that blood began pouring out of Him?

He went back to the chosen three. *They were fast asleep.* He called to them to wake up. Did they have any idea of what He was about to endure for them? Could they not stay awake with Him for one hour? He went back to the rock. Because of the agony Jesus suffered, this rock would later be called *The Rock of Agony.* He prayed hard.

His humanity had to have surfaced. He must have looked at these three, who had fallen asleep, and thought: They were the best of the lot, and *they* couldn't be depended on. To quote Archbishop Fulton J. Sheen, *"these were the ones He trusted to stay awake."* Was the time right? Was it too soon? Had He prepared them sufficiently? Would they be strong enough to carry on the work? After all, it had only been three years. These eleven were not the brightest, or best educated. They were simple men, for the most part fishermen. Jesus spoke frankly to the Father. He said,

"Father, if it be Your will, take this cup from Me; yet not My will but Yours be done."[9]

Jesus went back to the three apostles.   They were asleep, again. He woke them. He chided them: *"Why are you sleeping? Wake up, and pray that you may not be subjected to the trial."*[10]   But it was too late, now.   He could hear commotion not far off.   It was Judas and the soldiers from the chief priests, approaching.   According to plan, Judas embraced Jesus.   He looked at Judas with such love.   He knew He was about to be betrayed; but it didn't stop Him from loving His betrayer. Judas averted Jesus' eyes.   Jesus smiled sadly at His fallen apostle.   *"Judas, would you betray the Son of Man with a kiss?"*[11]

At this point, a riot broke out.   The soldiers went for Jesus; the apostles tried to stop them.   Peter, still not quite awake, pulled out a sword, and began flailing it through the air. It landed on one of the priest's servants, and severed his ear.   There was a hush.   Jesus grabbed Peter's hand, and stopped him.   *"Enough!"*   Then He touched the man's ear and healed him.

Jesus looked to those who were in charge, the priests, the chiefs of the temple guard, and the elders. He was *hurt*. What had He ever done to them, or to us?

"Am I a criminal," he asked, *"that you come out after Me armed with clubs and swords? When I was with you day after day in the temple, you never raised a hand against me."*[12]   He could see He was getting nowhere.   But He had to give it one last try.   He had to let them know what was happening. He said: *"But this is your hour - the triumph of darkness."*[13]

---

[9]Luke 22:42
[10]Matt 26:40-41
[11]Luke 22:48
[12]Matt 22:52-53
[13]Matt 22:53

I've often wondered about that last statement of Jesus in the Garden of Gethsemane. Who was it directed to? Was He speaking to the chief priests and temple guards, or was Satan lurking in the shadows that night? Had Satan's demons taken over the hearts of those who now wanted to see Jesus dead? Had they filled the priests' hearts with hate for Jesus, using them to do their evil work? We know that Lucifer is the prince of the world, the prince of darkness. Was Jesus speaking directly to him?

Things haven't changed much since the time of Jesus. Satan is still spewing out his hate and venom upon the world, using man to do his dirty work. And we have allowed ourselves to be suckered in so easily. Satan knows what buttons to push, to make us react just the way he would have us. And over the past two thousand years, we have systematically been destroying ourselves. Paul gave us an insight into the battle that has been raging down through the centuries. *"Put on the armor of God, that you may be able to stand firm against the tactics of the devil. For our struggle is not against flesh and blood; but against principalities and powers, against the world rulers of this present darkness, with the evil spirits in the heavens."*[14]

You cannot stand on the spot where Jesus prayed in the Garden of Gethsemane and not reflect on what Jesus might have been thinking and feeling. Straight ahead, directly across from where Jesus was praying and suffering, were the golden gates. It was through these gates that they had led Jesus *triumphantly*, the Sunday before (Palm Sunday). They had waved palms and laid them at His feet. Now, they wanted to kill Him. Was this part of Your pain, Jesus? Did You cry out: *"What did I do to you? I only wanted to love you, to heal you, to forgive you?"* Jesus, did You say, once again: *"Well, I Love you, I heal you, I forgive*

---

[14]Eph 6:11-13

you, even as you plan My death on the Cross."?   Forgive us, dear Lord.

This is the perfect time to put on the armor of God. We are possibly in the most crucial period of our Church, our country, and our world.   Only the anticipation of the triumph of the Cross can bring us through the forth-coming Passion of Our Lord.   As we approach the 21st century, if we do not realize that this is *his* (the devil's) *hour*, we are living in a fool's paradise.   We have only to read the papers, watch secular television to know that the battle is on!   As you view the scandalous behavior which is now purported to be the norm, as all our traditions are being desecrated and we watch dissension ripping families apart, Jesus' prophecy seems to be coming to pass before our very eyes:

"And when you hear of wars and revolutions, do not be frightened, for this is something that must happen but the end is not so soon....Nation will fight against nation, and kingdom against kingdom.   There will be great earthquakes and plagues and famines here and there; there will be fearful sights and great signs from Heaven.

"But before all this happens, men will seize you and persecute you; they will hand you over to the synagogues and to imprisonment, and bring you before kings and governors because of My Name....You will be betrayed even by parents and brothers, relatives and friends, and some of you will be put to death.   You will be hated by all men on account of My Name, but not a hair of your head will be lost.   Your endurance will win your lives."[15]

Our Lady (of Fatima) appeared to three children at the beginning of the twentieth century and she gave one of them, Lucia, the third secret which she told her to give to no one but the Pope.   Since then, Pope after Pope has read the Third Secret and not made it public.   Now, as the twentieth

---

[15]Luke 21:9-19

century is closing, the Lord has sent us a powerful Pope to lead his people to the Triumph of the Cross. Our dear Pope John Paul II is reaching out to his children, bringing them the Truth. Is the Third Secret the apostasy that threatens our Church from within and without? Is this what our dear Lord saw in the Garden of Gethsemane as He sweat Blood and Tears on the Rock of Agony? An Angel came to console the Lord. Are Angels coming to us to bring His Word to us? Be not afraid, we are with you, fighting by your side. The Cross will triumph!

How do we protect ourselves and our families against the powers of hell? We must become prayer warriors. Go to Daily Mass, not only during Lent, but the rest of your life. Your life and the lives of your loved ones depend on it. Pray, pray often. Receive the Sacraments. They are weapons of strength for us. Fasting and abstinence are means to strengthen our souls, and give prayer cover to the Angels to protect us from the evil one. Our Lord has given us these gifts to help us ward off the prince of this world.

Through these gifts, we can change the world, not by legislation, or by force, but by emptying our hearts, and allowing Him to fill us with His Holy Spirit. We must allow the Lord to break our hearts of stone, and make them into new creations of His Love. And when this happens, change will come about in us, and through us, the world.

We have a great opportunity to take some of the pressure off Jesus' Head in the Garden of Gethsemane. *Let's give up sinning!* If each of us commits one less sin, or gives up sinning altogether, at least some of that pain will be alleviated. If we give up sins, His suffering will be less. And we'll really feel pretty good about ourselves. *Try it! Do it!*

The Scourging at the Pillar

The gift of the Sorrowful Mysteries is different for each of us. Jesus speaks to every one of us *individually*. He desires to imprint on our hearts what is necessary and good for us. He comes to us and shares with us, so that we can better relate to Him. We all say we want to get to know Jesus better, to take a closer walk with Him. But do we mean His walk to the Pillar, to be scourged? Or is it the Jesus Who drew crowds with His preaching, teaching and healing, we wish to encounter, the popular Jesus?

If we truly love Jesus, we will weep often as we journey with Him through these Mysteries of the Holy Rosary. The greatest gift we can receive is that of being able to conceive the *Suffering and Crucifixion of Our Lord Jesus*. For it is only through His Suffering that we truly discover the tremendous love that Jesus has for us. We need to go beyond the scripture passages; we need to concentrate on what really happened. Then we will ache, as we zero in on the true meaning of the words; then and only then we will come to terms with the great Sacrifice, Our Lord made for us.

Our Bible is beautiful, but I'm afraid we've gotten too used to it. We take too much for granted. After having read it, or had it read to us for so many years, we become numbed to the reality of certain words. Their *truth* becomes prettily covered over by flower beds of poetic language. And if we are not careful, they become poetry, not life. Phrases like *"Scourged at the Pillar"*, *"Mocked and spit upon,"* *"stripped of His garments"* and *"crowned with thorns"* flow trippingly from the tongue, when actually they have deep, gashing, agonizing, blood curdling, very deadly meanings. Each time we have brought a Pilgrimage to the Holy Land, we have been given the sorrowful gift of seeing these words translated into *life*, as we experience *how* it happened, *when* it happened, *why* it happened, and the physical trauma it caused our dear Lord Jesus.

In the Dictionary of the Bible,[1] we are told that in the Roman law, there were two kinds of scourgings. One was by order of the magistrate, in his presence, as a punishment; it was like a slap on the wrist. This was called the *Verberatio*.

The other was the *Flagellatio*, or Flagellation, which was designed to torture and kill. The whips that were used were made with jagged animal bones tied to them, as a means of ripping the flesh from the body in clumps. They were also laced with metal balls, which were designed to splinter and break the prisoner's bones. Jesus suffered the Flagellation, and then some. *He revealed to St. Brigid that He received more than 5000 wounds at the hands of the Romans during the scourging.*

[The *Flagellatio was so brutal, so dehumanizing that the law severely prohibited the scourging of Roman citizens under any conditions.* This does not mean they were not subjected to it. Paul was scourged many times, by the Romans in spite of his Roman citizenship, and by the Jews just because he was Paul.]

---

[1]John L. McKenzie, S.J.- MacMillan Publishing Co., 1965

†

We have seen a statue of Jesus at the pillar in the church built over the home where St. Teresa of Avila was born. I have never been able to look at my Jesus *there*, tied to the pillar, and not weep. His back was covered with purple swollen welts and open bleeding, gaping wounds, precious flesh hanging limply from his body. He had not the Face of a grown Man, but the look of a sensitive, *young* Man. I still remember the day that our grandson Rob called us over to see this statue. He said that men from our pilgrimage were over there, and they were crying. When we approached, I could immediately see why. Those Eyes, we will never forget Your Eyes, Jesus! You looked so vulnerable, so abandoned. You did not look like a Man Who was wise with the ways of the world, who understood what was happening. You looked young and wounded! The Youth that was before us was more wounded in His Heart than on His Body. It was as if You were pleading with us, Jesus. You were asking what You had done wrong. Jesus, you were speaking to us, as You spoke to St. Teresa of Avila:

"Around 1555, someone brought to the Convent, a painting of Our Lord and Savior in His Passion, bleeding, bruised and broken. She (St.Teresa) *prostrated herself before Him, begging Him to release her from the bondage of the liar and his lies, with his false gifts of the world and the flesh. She asked His forgiveness for the many times she had foolishly been tempted by people and things of the world, 'My Lord and my God, I will not get up from here until you grant me this favor.' This was to be the turning point in Teresa's life. She had passionately prayed with her heart and soul, and the Savior responded, as He did when walking the Earth. 'Your faith has saved you. Your sins are forgiven. Pick up your mat and walk.' She had*

*fought the good fight and she had won! She was free, free
at last of the lure of the devil and his kingdom, the world."*[2]

St. Teresa saw Jesus at the pillar, Hands tied, as He
just stood there and let them scourge Him. We could not
forget the Eyes of Jesus that we saw on the statue. Neither
could Saint Teresa; she said her vocation was sealed the day
she saw Jesus come to life on that painting, and she was
never the same. She carried a small statue with her,
whenever she went to open a new house, of the Jesus Who
spoke to her and to Whom she spoke, in her vision. When
we look at this statue, we want to cry out with His Mother,
and St. Teresa, and all the Saints and Angels: *"Look at the
Face of Jesus. Look into His Eyes. Feel His open, gaping
wounds. Please do not make sport with Him, anymore."*

†

After they were finished with Jesus, the chief priests
and the scribes handed Jesus over to Pilate. When Judas
heard that our Lord had been condemned, he despaired and
hanged himself.

Pilate questioned Jesus: *"Are you the king of the Jews?"*
When Jesus said *"Mine is not a kingdom of this world..."*[3]
Pilate did not understand what He meant. With his worship
of power and earthly conquest, he had no idea what Jesus
was saying when He continued: *"But yes, I am a King."*

When Jesus said: *"I came into the world for this; to bear
witness to the truth; and all who are on the side of truth listen to
My Voice."* again Pilate did not understand. Not recognizing
his chance at redemption, he scornfully replied, *"Truth?
What is that?"*[4] How could Pilate have known what Jesus was
trying to teach him, since truth did not live in his heart. He

---

[2]taken from the chapter on St. Teresa of Avila in Bob and Penny
Lord's book: *"Saints and other Powerful Women in the Church."*
[3]John 18:36-37
[4]John 18:38

had long ago traded *truth* for the false gifts of glory and position.

Pilate turned to the people: "*I find no case against Him.*" Seeing he could not reach the mob, Pilate planned to have our Lord flogged and then release him. He thought when the crowd sees Jesus after his scourging, they will be moved to pity and he can let Him go.

There was a Roman game called the **King's Game.** The Roman soldiers tossed dice for a prisoner. The winner was given the prisoner for a week, during which time, he could torture and ridicule the prisoner as often as he wanted, in as many perverse ways as he chose. At the end of that week, he killed the prisoner. Jesus was turned over to the guards by Pontius Pilate for scourging. He became a pawn in the King's game. The crowning of thorns and shrouding with the purple cloak are parts of that game. When Pilate turned Him over to the guards, he did not anticipate that Jesus would be beaten near to death, though that was part of the game. As far as the guards were concerned, Jesus was merely a candidate for the King's game. The only difference was, they only had one day to torture Jesus, because He would be executed at the end of the day.

When Pilate saw Jesus, after He had endured this torture, he had to have been shocked. When he cried out, **"Ecce Homo! Behold the Man!"** he thought for sure, the priests and the scribes would be moved to release Jesus. He was completely staggered when they called for Jesus' death by crucifixion. Pilate may have been shocked, but not enough to resist the crowd when they shouted the louder, "*Crucify Him! Crucify Him!*" The tragedy was that it was not the majority, but a few well-placed agitators in the crowd who loudly coerced the rest to join them in condemning the Man Who had healed them, Who had brought them Good News, the One they had proclaimed the Messiah, the Sunday before. Do you condemn them? When the world shouts *Crucify Him*, do you go with the pace-setters of the world and say nothing? Will you say, when you face Jesus someday, "But Lord, when did I choose the world instead of You?" Will you look away, as He responds: *"What did you do, child, when they defamed My Immaculate and precious Mother? What did you say when they denied My existence? Did you just stand by and not get involved?"*

How many times dear Lord, how many times are You scourged for our sins? It's bad enough, You had to sacrifice Your Life for us, and die for our sins. Did we have to add insult to injury by having You mocked and beaten, in addition? Do we still drag You before the soldiers to have Your back laid bare, so that You can be tortured in such a barbaric, inhuman way? After having experienced the reality of what our dear Lord went through for us, you would think we would never ever even *consider* sinning again. When we realize that our sins put huge nails into His Body, pressed a Crown of razor sharp thorns onto His head, thorns so long they pierced His Skull, a whip of jagged animal bones and heavy metal balls lashing, cutting into His back, we could never sin. Right? *Wrong!*

We are an *Alleluia* people. We are a *Resurrection* people. We are an Easter Sunday people. But in order to appreciate the joy of Alleluia, and the gifts of Resurrection, we must first experience the rejection, the suffering and the Crucifixion. In order to really understand what "*Happy Days are Here Again*" means, we must grasp fully what men jumping off roofs of tall buildings and smashing their bodies into heaps on the streets below during the Depression meant. "*Brother, can you spare a dime?*" (another song of the Depression) is not romantic, when you are starving so badly, you're ready to eat a dog.

We have a great opportunity. We can *listen* to the Scripture passages and *visualize* them as they relate to the torture and death of Our Lord Jesus. We can personalize them. We can pay attention to them *this time*, so that perhaps we can take some of the blows that struck our Lord's Back. Perhaps we can take one of those jagged bones into our own flesh by doing without something which will lead us into sin, or by helping someone in need when we just don't want to do it. Maybe we can take one of the thorns that pierced His Skull into our skull, by rooting out some of those just plain rotten thoughts from our minds.

We praise You, dear Lord Jesus; we bless Your Holy Name. We thank You for suffering for us. We thank You for dying for us. We ask You to give us the strength we need to end our part in Your suffering. We pray that we never be the cause of one whiplash striking Your precious Body, that we never cause the pressure for one thorn to implant itself into Your beautiful Head. If I, Lord, by disciplining myself can take away one moment of pain from You, and if others, by my example can take away a moment, and others and others, we will truly see a New Jerusalem, where the old days and the old ways are replaced by a new world, where the lion will truly lie down with the lamb, and there will be no more bloody sacrifices. For us men, nothing is possible. *For God, all things are possible.*

The Crowning of Thorns

Everybody wants to go to Heaven, but nobody wants to die. Everybody wants the Resurrection, but nobody wants the Crucifixion. That has been the story of Salvation History in general, but the I-centered Twentieth Century in particular. We are coming out of a century, where everyone grabbed whatever he could for himself, no matter who it hurt, or how it affected our country or our world.

We know, Jesus did not want to die. He asked His Father in the Garden of Gethsemane, *"If it be Your will, let this cup pass from Me."* He could have given His Father thousands of reasons why He should stay on the earth a little longer. He didn't want to die, but He said yes! *"Yet not My will, but Yours be done."* There it was: that's what made Satan so furious, that complete **Yes**, that unconditional **Yes**, that **Yes** with full knowledge of the consequences.

†

Pilate, unable to move their hearts of stone, ordered our most precious Lord to be taken away. *"The soldiers led Him away to the Praetorium. Then they stripped Him and dressed Him up in purple."*[1] They twisted some thorns into a crown and pressed it down, piercing His Head. Further mocking Him, they placed a reed in His Hand, to represent a scepter. They contemptuously knelt before Him, hailing Him *King of the Jews*. When that sport ceased to entertain

---

[1]Mark 15:16-17

91

them, they took the reed from His Hand and struck Him, with it, over and over again on His Head. They spit at Him.

They mocked Him; they accused Him; and He was silent, never defending Himself, paying with His silence the ransom for our sins. Lord, they stripped You of all Your garments. They derided You. They taunted You, those who were not worthy to kiss Your Feet. And You did nothing!

No one wants Jesus to suffer; it calls us to accountability. If He could do it, we have the responsibility to do it, also. No one wants Jesus to stand by and do nothing, say nothing. Does that mean when someone falsely accuses me, Lord, I am to do and say nothing? *"But He was God!"* We love to shout that. I can hear Jesus crying out *"But I was man also. I was like you in all things except Sin."* We have to come to terms with the fact Jesus suffered *physically*. He endured all the pain we go through. We can't hide behind the fact that Jesus was God. He was Man, too.

So that there is no doubt in anyone's mind how much your Savior, the God-Man Who gave up His life for His friends and His enemies, suffered, we need to look at *Jesus Crowned with Thorns*! His suffering was more severe than ours, because He was taking on the sins of the world. He was suffering for all the sins which had been committed before Him, all that went on during His lifetime, and the tens of billions of sins which would be committed in the future.

How painful was that Crown on His Head? When our Lord appeared to St. Margaret Mary Alacoque, He told her that His *enemies* placed a Crown of Thorns on His Head, His *friends* on His Heart. Are we the friends who place a Crown around His Heart, today? As He looked about the crowd, at those He had touched, those He had healed, those to whom He had brought hope, those who repaid His Love by running away, who denied Him out of fear, was a second Crown placed, on His Heart?

In the Western World, we're at a disadvantage. We cannot visualize a thorn so big, it could penetrate a skull, and inflict fatal injuries. We know of little thorns from rose bushes; they draw blood and inflict excruciating pain, but are nothing compared to the spear-like thorns in the Holy Land.

We were at the Shrine of the Miracle of the Eucharist in Bois Seigneur Isaac, in Belgium, this summer. In the same Chapel which holds the Miraculous bloodstained Corporal, there is a reliquary of one of the thorns from the Crown of Thorns our Lord wore. It was about four inches long, and razor-sharp. The thorns which pierced the Head of our dear, innocent Savior, were that long and that sharp. When we go on pilgrimage to the Shrine of St. Rita, in Cascia, we meditate on the thorn that came from our Lord's Cross and pierced her forehead; it was 4 inches long!

When you journey to the Holy Land during Holy Week, you see replicas of the Crown of Thorns that Jesus wore. It is difficult to look at; reality always is. You want to turn away. Surely, Lord they did not press this crown of thorns on Your precious Head. But they did! If *we* can never forget that replica of His Crown, what painful memories did Mother Mary have to deal with, as she remained on earth doing her Heavenly Father's Will?

Each year, when we bring our pilgrims to the Chapel of St. Bridget in the Basilica of St. Paul, outside the Walls of Rome, we share the conversations Jesus had with St. Bridget of Sweden. He not only described how many wounds He received, as the soldiers struck Him over and over again, while tied to the pillar, He shared how one of the thorns from the Crown, the soldiers pressed down on His Head, pierced the top of His Head and came out through His forehead. *It would have to have actually penetrated His skull!* Jesus told St. Bridget that this was a fatal thorn, a fatal blow. Had He not been crucified, He would have died from this wound.

Early icons of our Lord Jesus depict Him with what seems to be a little curl, a wisp of hair, coming down from His forehead. This is not a lock of hair. In actuality, it is the thorn extruding from His head. If you look at the image of the Holy Shroud, the wound of one of the thorns is visible.

We want the clean, white, gleaming Jesus. A woman once came up to Penny, and tried to rip her crucifix from her neck. She screamed, *"Take Him off the Cross. Why do you have to keep reminding us of the Cross?"* Nobody wants that thorn to stick out from His head; they want it to be a lock of hair. Our brothers and sisters, not of the Roman Catholic Faith worship the Risen Christ. Martin Luther could not come to terms with the Crucified Christ. Jesus accepted the call to the Crucifixion; Luther could not. Jesus obeyed and we were saved; Luther disobeyed and gave birth to the greatest *Scandal of the Cross* our Church has ever known. But as Jesus saved His Church once through the Cross, so He does it, over and over again. That's why we can't run from the Cross. Our *Salvation* is through that Cross.

"Pick up your Cross, and follow Me." We are all given crosses. They are designed especially for us, unlike the one our dear Lord Jesus had to carry. They are just the right height and weight. They are fashioned to fit perfectly, because we have been given just enough grace to carry them. *"My grace is enough for you."*[2] Accept your cross; no, embrace your cross. You don't want anyone else's cross. It wouldn't fit. You wouldn't have enough grace to carry it.

When our nineteen year old son died of an overdose of drugs, we were devastated. We thought no other cross could be as heavy, or as painful. We didn't think we could carry it. We felt like we were crumbling under the weight of it, until we met a person who had just lost a spouse. When that person told us she could never carry *our* cross, we

---

[2]2Cor 12:9

realized that we would collapse under the weight of her cross. God never gives us a cross we cannot carry.

We are not heroes. Please believe me, we don't want to suffer; we don't want to die. We don't want to experience physical pain, much less emotional or spiritual pain. We want the Resurrection. We want that clean Jesus, dressed in brilliant white, with not a wound on Him. But that's not the way it works. We know we can't have that Resurrection without the Crucifixion. But we say, "*How, Lord? How can I endure that pain, that suffering? How can I let a thorn the size of a nail, be pounded through my skull? I'm not strong enough for that.*" What is the answer? I want to know as well.

We were on *Mother Angelica Live* a few months ago. A woman called in and asked what the meaning of *Signal Grace* was. Mother defined Signal Grace as a special grace given for a special need. She used as an example, the early Christian martyrs, who waited their turn at the Colosseum and the Circus Maximus, as they witnessed their brothers and sisters being torn to pieces by the ravenous animals. They waited and sang songs in praise of Our Lord Jesus. *That took Signal Grace.* Mother Angelica mentioned St. Maxmilian Mary Kolbe, a Saint of the Twentieth Century, who gave up his life, in the death camp of Auschwitz, Poland in 1941, so that another might live. When he went up to the Nazi officer in charge, and made his request, it took *Signal Grace* to give up his life for a perfect stranger. *Pick up your Cross and follow Me. My grace is enough for you.*

An afflicted Jesus was brought before Pontius Pilate. A Crown of thorns had been jokingly placed on His bleeding Head, a purple cloak draped mockingly on His wounded Shoulders; blood and sweat poured forth from His scourged Flesh; Pilate wanted nothing to do with Jesus. This had gone too far. Lord, how did the mob dare to look upon Your suffering? How could those You had healed, those You had forgiven, how could they been a party to Your humiliation?

"*Ecce Homo!*" Pontius Pilate cried out, "*Behold the Man.*" He was hoping for some sympathy, some remorse from the crowd. After all, they had been His followers; they had pursued Him from place to place; they had hailed Him, just the Sunday before, as He entered Jerusalem. But the crowd was deaf to his plea. They had been stirred up into a wild, angry frenzy. I believe that some were even too afraid to defend Jesus. The violent *few* have always been able to intimidate the frightened *many* into doing their will. "*Away with Him; crucify Him!*" they shouted. When we choose the world and its acceptance before Jesus, are we not rejecting Him? When we just stand by while the very vocal *few* take over and shout "*Crucify Him!*" are we not shouting "*Crucify Him*" by our silence?

Pontius Pilate's wife had had a dream. She sent word to her husband to have nothing to do with the death of this Innocent Man. It was a Feast Day of the Jews. At this time, Pilate would allow them to choose a prisoner to be released. They chose a murderer and thief. "*Give us Barabbas! Give us Barabbas!*" Whom do we choose? When we vote for preservation of our comforts, instead of preservation of human life, whom do we choose? Who is our Barabbas?

Then Pilate, seeing the crowd's unrelenting condemnation of Jesus, took some water, and turning to the people, washed his hands, saying "*I am innocent of this man's blood. It is your concern.*"[3] To a man, they all shouted: "*His Blood be on us, and on our children.*" Oh, Lord, how very often the sins of the parents are suffered by the children. Today, when we are being told that anything goes, and then we wake up to see the innocent lives that are suffering, the babies infected with AIDS because one or both of his parents bought into that lie, it makes us tremble. Oh, Lord, not the innocent children. Let it stop, now!

---

[3]Matt 27:24

When Pilate asked what harm Jesus had done, what could they have replied - He healed us; He forgave our sins so we could start over; He brought us the Bread of Life; He fed us in body and spirit? What could they have answered? *"Crucify Him!"* they shouted all the louder. Jesus was the Light. With His Light, He brought to light all the sins that had been done in darkness. When they condemned others, He revealed to them *their* sins, cautioning them not to judge lest they be judged. They couldn't be superior, couldn't look down on anyone with Jesus present; He knew all there was to know about *them*. They had to silence Him. *Crucify Him!*

Are we a party to our Lord's walk to His death? A young man once asked Penny, how she felt about the Nuns having a Convent outside of Auschwitz? When she asked what the problem was, he said it was a reminder to the Jews that Christians killed 6,000,000 Jews. Penny said *"No Christians killed Jews at Auschwitz or anywhere else. Godless Nazis did."* "Well," he said, "the Germans just watched and did nothing." *"Oh, then Germans were accountable because they just watched their Jewish brothers and sisters go by in trains at night, to death camps? Were these Christians condemned for standing by, doing nothing to try to stop it?"* Penny then asked him if we, the people of the United States, are accountable for watching our innocents go to *our* American death camps, the Abortion Clinics? Are we not condemned for standing by, and doing nothing? He replied, he didn't get involved in such things. She said: *"Neither did the Germans."*

Forgive us Jesus; we don't want You bleeding and dirty; we don't want a Crown of thorns on Your Head. We want to see You as *Christ the King* with a gold crown on Your Head, victorious. We don't really want to look upon You and the Cross. You told us to pick up our Cross and follow You, that Salvation was through the Cross. But it's so hard. *Forgive us, Jesus, we know not what we do. Or do we?*

Jesus Carries His Cross

The Long Road to Calvary

John cried out, a lone voice in the desert:

"Prepare the way of the Lord; make straight His paths."[1]
He cried out! He didn't speak, as if it was a passing thought
like: "Oh by the way, did you know the Lord is coming?" *He
cried out! He cried! There was urgency! There was passion!*
He was risking his *life* to proclaim the Lord's coming. When
he came out to the desert, and began to tell everyone to
repent, he was on the way to his death. Why did he do it?
He had no choice. Only God can give that kind of courage;
and John the Baptist had known the Lord from the time he
was inside his mother's womb. *"When Elizabeth heard Mary's
greeting, the baby leapt in her womb."*[2]

Did John know what kind of road they would prepare
for the Lord? Did he ever, for one moment, consider it
could be the Road to Calvary? God, the Father in Heaven
did not reveal the whole plan to John. If He had, would
John have been able to lay the groundwork for our Lord's
first coming? He told everyone who would listen, to repent.
Did those who were present, that joyful day, hear with their
heads and act through their hearts? Did John's words find a
place in their lives? When Jesus was baptized by John in the
River Jordan and the Father's words descended from
Heaven: *"This is My beloved Son. My favor rests on Him."*,[3]

---

[1]Matt 3:3
[2]Luke 1:41
[3]Matt 3:17

was a thorn planted in their hearts? Then, why did they, three years later, place a Crown of thorns on His Head?

Our Lord received word that John had been beheaded, *John*, His messenger and dear cousin, the one who recognized Him, while He was still in His Mother's womb. He was dead! What did Jesus do? He went away to pray. Did He grieve? Had He seen the good that John could have continued doing and was now silenced? Or did He know in His Heart of hearts that John had lived for one purpose and that was to proclaim His coming, to pave the way for Him, the Redeemer, to save the world? John's words, *"He must increase while I must decrease."*,[4] were they coming to pass? Did Jesus grieve for the loss to the world of this great prophet? Did the Father come to Him and prepare Him for His total mission?

When did Jesus begin His way of the Cross? Was it at Cana, the night His Mother turned to Him and said *"They have no wine"*? Was it when He performed His first miracle, changing the water into wine? Was Jesus trying to tell His Mother that if He does that, the world will begin to know Who He is, His walk will begin, and life as they have known it, will be no more? Was that really what He was saying when He answered His Mother: *"Woman why turn to Me? My hour has not come yet"*?[5] Was Jesus trying to buy one more night of normality before starting His Ministry and His long journey to the Cross? Did Mother Mary understand that she was asking Him to begin the journey that could only end up at Calvary? Could she have still said *"Do whatever He tells you."*? And now, she still is saying the same thing, really, at every apparition, basically *"Do whatever He tells you."*

Jesus had been teaching. He had been travelling the countryside healing the mind, the spirit, the body, the heart.

---

[4]John 1:30
[5]John 2:4

He had been leading His children gently, holding them by the hand, along the path to understanding the Father's Will in their lives. He warned them, they could not have two masters; they would hate the one and love the other. He cautioned them not to judge one another. He brought them hope with His Words: "*Ask, and you will receive; seek and you will find; knock and the door will be opened to you.*" He also made them uncomfortable. The people in towns where He performed many miracles did not turn from their sins and so He chastised them, telling them: "*I assure you that on Judgment Day, God will show more mercy to the people of Tyre and Sidon than to you.*"[6] But he never gave up on them, patiently and compassionately, consistently reaching out to them. He tried to reach them: "*Do you think what I am asking of you is too difficult?*" Knowing their pain, He reassured them: "*Come to Me all of you who are tired from carrying heavy loads and I will give you rest.*"[7]

Knowing His time was near, and they would never make it without His Presence among them, He gave them Food for the journey. It has been said that the Church would not have lasted one hundred years without the Eucharist. When Jesus believed they were ready, or was it more that He knew His hour had come, He prepared them for the Gift of the Holy Eucharist. When He fed more than five thousand men *(they did not count women and children in those days)* with five loaves and two fish, they loved Him! They wanted more, and so they followed Him. They found Him praying in a synagogue in Capharnaum. *Then* He made the decision that began His walk to the Cross; He proclaimed the Eucharistic Doctrine: "*I am the Bread of Life. He who comes to Me will never go hungry; he who believes in Me will never be thirsty.*"[8] Most of those who had followed

---

[6]Luke 10:14
[7]Matt:11:28
[8]John 6:35

Him, left; hence Jesus began His lonely walk to the Cross.
Then He asked His chosen twelve "*Will you leave Me, too?*",
and one of them (Judas) began to plot against Him.

Why did those *from* whom He had come, and *for*
whom He had come, (the chosen people) leave? Why did
Judas betray Him? Bishop Sheen said our Lord's teaching
on the Eucharist was too much for them to bear, and so they
killed Him. Was it too simple? Did it require too much
faith? Did His teaching now lack the excitement, the
sensationalism they had found in the miracles He had
performed in their midst? It began with grumbling; it ended
with Crucifixion. Jesus scolded them: "Stop your grumbling!"
"*I am the Living Bread that comes down from Heaven. If
anyone eats this Bread he will live forever. The Bread that I will
give is My Flesh for the life of the world.*"⁹ They did not
understand; they did not know Him; they did not want Him
any longer. They had had expectations of Him that He
would not fulfill; they would silence him. They could no
longer look upon Him. They wanted Him to disappear, and
so they killed Him.

Jesus began to form and prepare His Church. He
asked His followers, first, "*Who do people say that I am?*"¹⁰
They gave Him multiple answers: Elijah, John the Baptist,
still others Jeremiah or one of the prophets. Then Jesus
turned to the Apostles: "*Who do you say I am?*"¹¹ Peter
professed: "*You are the Messiah, the Son of the living God.*"¹²
Knowing Peter's wisdom was not from man, but had been
revealed to him by His Heavenly Father, Jesus proclaimed
him *rock* and declared that upon *him* He would build *His*
Church. Jesus, at that very moment in time, chose Peter as
His first Pope. And even after Peter denied Him three

⁹John 6:51
¹⁰Matt 16:13
¹¹Matt 16:15
¹²Matt 16:16

times, Jesus did not take back His Mission from Peter. For Jesus always did the Will of His Father in Heaven. Knowing this was His Father's Will, He gave an irrevocable *yes!* And so, with His Yes, not only did Jesus found His Church, but the *Holy Trinity*, One and inseparable, *created* her. The *world* was given Mother Church, and would know her, after she flowed from the Bleeding Heart of our Savior on the Cross.

On the way to Jerusalem, Jesus ascended Mount Tabor, bringing Peter, James and John with Him. It was so breathtaking, so beautiful, so peaceful up there, on this mountain high above the patchwork fields, away from all the problems below. The Lord showed them His Glorious Self: *"As they looked on, a change came over Jesus: His Face was shining like the sun, and His clothes were dazzling white."*[13] Peter, James and John heard a Voice descending from Heaven: *"This is My own dear Son, with Whom I am pleased - listen to Him!"*[14] Peter was so excited, he wanted to pitch tent up there: *"Lord how good it is for us to be here!"*[15] Would he have been so eager, so elated if he had known this was Jesus' way of preparing them, strengthening them for the walk through the valley to the next high place, Calvary?

The walk to Calvary had to be a lonely one. Jesus had tried to prepare His disciples: *"I will be put to death, but three days later I will be raised to life."*[16] Like so many of us, Peter did not hear: *"I will be raised to life."* The enemy of fear and uncertainty deafened his ears to Jesus' consoling, reassuring words. All Peter could say was: *"God forbid it, Lord!"*[17] As You, Jesus, saw Your first Pope weaken so many times, as You see us disappoint You with our own needs and agendas, how do You stick with us, Lord?

---

[13]Matt 17:2
[14]Matt 17:5
[15]Matt 17:4
[16]Matt 17:22
[17]Matt 16:22

†

Our biggest enemy is *fear*, Lord. Fear is the reason Peter denied You three times, fear of pain and death. Today, the world is very busily engaged in spreading fear and hopelessness. One of our local priests said, the other day, during his homily: "Over the gates of hell, there is a sign which reads *'Abandon hope all you who enter.'*" Well, that's not where we want to end up. We definitely do not want to take any road that might lead us there.

So, now that we know the enemy's game, what do you say we walk beside Jesus and take up our own cross, as we prepare for the Resurrection, and the Glorious Mysteries. Whenever we are tempted to ask the question "*Why me, Lord?*" we need only to open the New Testament and read the life of Jesus. We will discover the Way of the Cross started *before* Jesus entered Jerusalem. And as we then start to meditate on our own walk, we will meet that Precious Savior who has been walking beside us all our life, and if we dare look upon Him, we will bless Him for our life and all that has happened, is happening and will happen.

Our modern theology tells us that when we sin, we break relationship with Jesus, and I'm sure that's true, and upsetting. But if we come to terms with the fact that when we sin, we take our foot, and kick Him with all our might, in His Side, as He's carrying the cross, that our sins might just have been the catalyst to make Him buckle under and crumble, bloody, face-first onto the ground, if we love Him the way we say we do, we have to want to cut off our leg, before sinning against Him. And yet, we sin and sin and sin.

†

When Jesus walked along the Via Dolorosa (the Way of the Cross), the soldiers poked Him, prodding Him, although He needed no prodding. He fell three times, Face down into the dirt, weighed down by the Cross. But He got up! On Pilgrimage, whenever we walk the Way of the Cross and I behold my Lord, alone and abandoned, the weight of the Cross crushing Him, looking up at me, with such a look of *human* helplessness, I want to shout: "*Don't get up, Lord. Stay down! No more, Lord. Don't let them hurt You, anymore. Why do You get up? Is it so that when I don't want to begin again, when I don't want to carry my cross, I will remember You, weighed down by the Cross, getting up, going on to Your Death?*"

There was no one to help You carry Your Cross, Jesus. No one considered it a privilege or honor to take Your Cross from Your Shoulders. Simon of Cyrene had to be forced into helping You with Your Cross. Peter stood a safe distance away, to avoid confrontation, pain and possibly death.

†

I have had a desire to be like Mother Mary, ever since I discovered Bob loved and admired her so. Sadly, I knew, I was more like my patron saint, St. Paul, than Mother Mary. Be careful what you pray for; you might get your wish. One year, during Holy Week, at twelve noon on Good Friday, we were standing at Calvary, in Jerusalem, on the side, watching the Greek Orthodox Patriarch and his pilgrims process by, carrying the Cross. They had been walking about 15 across. Now, as they were approaching the entrance to the Church of The Holy Sepulchre (where Calvary is) the road became narrow, barely three deep. I was so enthralled with the procession, I was not aware that my grandson was in danger until I heard Bob crying out: "*Robbie, they're crushing you!*" I whirled around. Our grandson's face was red like fire. He looked as if all the breath was being squeezed out of him. He was being crushed! I began to swing my arms in an attempt to push through pilgrims who had suddenly become a wall of menacing impenetrable bodies. I was blind and oblivious to everything and everyone but saving my grandson. Suddenly, I heard a voice: "*I'm on your side.*" It was my Bob. I had been punching my Bob, and not even knowing it, in an attempt to save my grandson. All of a sudden, I looked around. I thought: *Is this where Jesus met up with Mother Mary? Is this where she said Yes, one more time?* Is this where she said nothing, but said so much with her silence. Did her eyes say: "*It's all right, Son, I say Yes. I love you and I do not know how I will live without you, but I know this is what You have to do, and I say Yes.*" I started to weep. Well, I wanted to be more like Mother Mary, and Jesus was showing me how very far I would have to walk. Mother Mary, how did you do it?

†

We knew a family who was losing their ten year old daughter to cancer. They were a model family of hope and love. One time, when we visited them, it was the little girl's birthday. The family propped her on a bean bag chair on the floor. She could not see and could barely hear, but all the members of their church came and knelt in front of her, bringing her gifts. We could not hold back our tears; it reminded us so of the Baby Jesus in the manger.

The father used to call us almost every day. One night, more into the wee hours of the next morning, he called; he apologized; he said he couldn't sleep. He cried, he just couldn't carry his cross that night; it was too heavy. I asked him if he would invite Jesus into his home. Would he allow Jesus to help him with his cross? I told him that Jesus was not an apathetic bystander. He was very involved in his life. He did not have to be prodded, as had Simon, who reluctantly helped Jesus carry *His* Cross. Why didn't he hand his cross to Jesus? I told him that the Lord would love to help him. Now this daddy was a simple faith-filled soul. He said *yes*, he would, and we both hung up. The next morning, he called and said he had done what I had suggested. He said his arm hurt so badly, he could hardly raise it. I asked him what had he done. He answered:

"When I asked Jesus to carry my cross, what could I do but carry His."

[There is a P.S. to this story. Although this family was Baptist, they called the Pope *their* Pope. They wondered if we knew Pope John Paul II, and if we could write to him and ask him to pray for their little girl. We said, we didn't know the Pope personally, no more than any other Catholic, but we would be glad to write. The Pope's letter to us, promising to pray for the little girl and the family, arrived on the Feast Day of St. Jude, October the 28th, the day the little girl died. It meant so much to the family, they gave the letter to the local newspaper, who promptly printed it.]

†

Lord, only the women dared to walk with You to the Cross. Oh, Veronica, what did you see in the eyes of Jesus as you wiped the Blood and Sweat from His most Precious Face? Oh women of Jerusalem, did you know what our Lord was talking about, as He told you to cry not for Him but for yourselves and your children. Oh Lord, what did You see at that moment? Were those women of Jerusalem standing in for the women of the world who would hold the lifeless bodies of *their* children in their arms, victims of a world that considers life so expendable?

Are you one of those women who Jesus was speaking to? Is He talking about your children? Is He asking you to look around and see what kind of a world, what kind of a country, what kind of a Church we are leaving to them? Is our Lord walking alone, as schools, secular television and the world take Him out of our children's lives? Will our children know Him, after we are gone? Do our children know Him, now? Was our Jesus talking to us? Is He talking to us, today? Is He crying out to us, in pain, as He carries the Cross of those millions of babies that are being so brutally killed-for-profit?

You say, you were not born when Jesus walked the Way of the Cross, abandoned by everyone but His Mother, St. John and some women. Do I hear you say you would not have stood by when they crucified our Lord, when they mocked and spit upon Him? How much a part of the Mass are you? Is your mind wandering back to the *business* of life? When you see someone leaving the altar area with the Lord in their hands, obviously unaware of Who it is they are holding, no less what to do with this most precious Host, our Lord truly present: *Body and Blood, Soul and Divinity*, do you just sit there, not wanting to bring attention to yourself? After all what if you are wrong; you wouldn't want to hurt anyone's *feelings*, or be embarrassed.

Is Jesus not your Brother? Is He not your Affair? When someone, whether in print, at the movies or on television, or in your presence mocks Him, criticizes His Church, His Word, the Commandments He laid down, attacks His most Holy and Beloved Mother do you stay politely silent, uninvolved? Bishop Sheen said that those who stood apathetically by while our Lord walked His Way to the Cross and hung there breathing His last Breath, hurt Him more than those who drove the nails into His Hands and Feet, wounded Him more than those who spit upon Him, pierced His Heart more painfully than the centurion whose sight was restored when he placed the Lord's precious Blood on his eyes.

Our Lord Jesus asks us: *"Can you not spend one hour with Me?"* Respond *yes*, and then head toward the Tabernacle in your church where Jesus is waiting, no, *longing* for you.

Are you a spectator during the Sacrifice of the Mass? *The Mass is not a spectator sport!* Or are you an active participant? For you see before you, your Lord and Savior, the same Crucified Lord, that same Jesus Who was born to die for us, coming to life on the Altar through the priest's calling upon the Holy Spirit and his consecrated hands. You witness the Crucifixion and the Resurrection of your Lord, Who is once again interceding with the Father for the redemption of your sins and my sins. And if you do not feel tears rushing to your eyes, then there is no life in you. You do not know Him. Be not surprised if someday He says to you: "*I do not know you.*"

Our brothers and sisters, we love you with the Hearts of Jesus and Mary. *Live* these Sorrowful Mysteries, not only during Lent, but every day of your life. Enter into His Heart and consecrate yourselves and your whole family to Him and His Beloved Mother through His Sacred Heart and her Immaculate Heart. Journey with Him and His Mother on the Way of the Cross. You say, you want a personal relationship with Jesus? Will you get to know Him through the Cross? If you say Yes, as He did, then you will experience the joy and exhilaration of an ongoing Resurrection, not only on Easter Sunday, but on all the Easter days, the Lord has prepared for you.

†

We want to leave you with a prayer Padre Pio prayed before the Crucifix where he received the Stigmata in San Giovanni Rotondo, Italy:

> "*You call Me the Way   but you don't follow Me*
> *You call Me the Light   but you don't see Me*
> *You call Me the Teacher   but you don't listen to Me*
> *You call Me the Lord   but you don't serve Me*
> *You call Me the Truth   but you don't believe in Me*
>   *Don't be surprised if one day I don't know you.*"

†

Jesus Dies on the Cross

"'If you're the Son of God, come down from that Cross. Come down and we'll believe.' Sure they will believe; they'll believe anything, just no Cross. No mortification, no self-denial." The shrill, piercing cry of the aging Archbishop Fulton J. Sheen ricocheted off the walls of the Church of St. Agnes, in New York City, on Good Friday, April 8, 1977. He continued, *"Many say 'I'll believe anything! I'll believe He's divine! I will believe in His Church; I will believe in His pontiff, only no Cross! no sacrifice!'"*

Archbishop Fulton J. Sheen said *"George Bernard Shaw said of the Cross; 'It's that that bars the way.' Sure it bars the way. It bars the way to hell!"* Could Archbishop Sheen see what was coming upon him, and us, full steam? Could he see the suffering, our Lord Jesus would have to undergo at the hands of those who claimed to love Him? In his last years, when he gave his most powerful retreats to priests, did the Lord give him an insight into the *real Agony* Jesus suffered in the Garden, the *real Agony* He suffered on the Cross: the *Agony* of the great Apostasy, which would take hold so strongly in our Church towards the end of the Twentieth Century? Is that why he cried out so painfully for his Lord, Who is tortured so terribly, by those who love Him?

†

The walk to Calvary would have been devastating for anyone, but for Jesus, Who had received mortal wounds twice that day, from the crown of thorns, and again from the scourging He received from the Roman guards, it had to be *pure agony!* By all that's right, He should have been mercifully dead before arriving at the top of this hill.

Our Savior was stripped of His tunic. He was thrown to the ground. Nails - blunt, huge nails more like flat-head spikes were pounded into His Hands and Feet. The pain was unbearable, but Jesus said yes with His silence. [We were present at a Passion Play and the actor who played our Lord cried out in agony, as the soldiers pounded each nail into His Precious Body.] Did You cry out, Jesus as they pierced Your Hands with nails - Hands that had healed, Hands that had reached out to love us, Hands that had welcomed sinners, Hands that had multiplied 5 loaves and 2 fish into enough food to feed close to 15,000 people on the Mount of Beatitudes? Now they were nailing those Hands to a Cross! No more would You heal us, love us, feed us. Wrong! Even as You were bleeding from the excruciating Wounds inflicted on Your Precious Hands, You were setting into motion the ongoing use of Your Hands through the anointed hands of Your Priests and Your faithful followers. Oh Lord, "*I adore the Wounds on Your Sacred Head with sorrow deep and true. May every thought I have today be an act of love for You.*"

"*I adore the Wounds on Your Sacred Hands with sorrow deep and true. May every work of my hands today be an act of love for You.*

"*I adore the Wounds on Your Sacred Feet with sorrow deep and true. May every step I take today be an act of love for You.*

"*I adore the Wounds on Your Sacred Heart with sorrow deep and true. May every beat of my heart today be an act of love for You.*"[1]

Jesus did not fit the cross He was given; it belonged to another. His Body had to be stretched to fit the cross; one of His Shoulders was pulled out of its socket and was

---

[1]Bob and Penny's beloved friend and former Pastor, Msgr. Thomas O'Connell, St. Jude's, Westlake Village, California, recites this prayer at every Mass during the Communion meditation.

dislocated.[2] Did You cry out as they inflicted yet another Wound, my dearest Jesus? Was every muscle, every nerve, every fiber of Your Noble Body crying out in silent agonizing pain? Could it have been any worse? Our Lord told St. Brigid of Sweden that He received 5480 blows during His Passion. It's impossible to comprehend anyone receiving over five thousand blows to their body, and not dying.

St. Bernard of Clairvaux asked the Lord which was His greatest suffering. Our Lord answered Him, "*I had on My shoulder, while I bore My cross on the way of sorrow, a most grievous wound which was more painful to Me than the others, and which is not recorded by men because they knew not of it. Honor this wound with thy devotion and I will grant thee whatsoever thou dost ask through its virtue and merits. And in regard of all those who shall venerate this wound, I will remit to them all.*" Was that the shoulder they later dislocated, Lord, which caused you so much pain? Do we continue to inflict pain on the most wounded parts of Your Body, the Church, as we refuse to take our place on the way to the Cross, as our Church is maligned and the Truth is distorted?

Jesus was lifted on the Cross, and left there to die. Jesus said to Nicodemus, "*As Moses lifted up the serpent, so must the Son of Man be lifted up.*" As the serpent did not have poison in it, although it looked poisonous, so Jesus, who looked guilty to those who chose to see guilt in Him, was without sin. And as all who looked at the serpent of brass were healed, so all who look at Our Lord on the Cross will be healed of the poison of sin. Every blow Jesus suffered was in payment for all the sins that had ever been, or ever would be. When you are weary and feel you cannot go another step, cannot endure another pain, or

---

[2]This is the result of testing that was done by NASA (National Aeronautical and Space Administration) on the Holy Shroud. P.S this has not been disproved by Carbon-dating. Instead Carbon-dating as exact scientific testing has been disproved.

disappointment, when you feel all is hopeless, look upon Hope on the Cross, on He Who died that you and your loved ones would be one day with Him in Paradise.

When compared with the rest of Jesus' Life, the Gospel writers didn't go deeply into the Crucifixion and Death of Our Lord Jesus. To our knowledge, two of the Gospel writers were not there, when our Lord died on the Cross. St. Mark, Scripture tells us, is believed to have witnessed the Crucifixion: "*And a certain young man followed Him, having a linen cloth cast about his naked body; and they laid hold of him.*"[3] And we know that St. John was there with Jesus' Mother. Did the others *not* write more, because they had not witnessed the Crucifixion of our Lord *first-hand*? Or was the Cross the problem? Was the Crucifixion a Scandal or a Triumph? It was almost as if it were a part of the life and ministry of their Lord that they didn't want to remember. They did speak about His being mocked, tantalized, degraded as no other before Him. They did recall Jesus' suffering and Humanity as He cried out, "*My God, My God, why have you deserted me?*" But it was only John, who had been at the foot of the Cross and suffered with Jesus' Mother, who saw the Cross as a *Triumph* and he wrote about it in this way.

Only *St. Luke* mentions that Jesus asked the Father to forgive His murderers. "*Forgive them Father, for they know not what they do.*"[4] Was this because this was important to *Mother Mary*? Was she telling *all* her children that Jesus forgave them and died that they might be forgiven their sins?

It is St. Luke who mentions the discourse between Jesus and the two thieves, and Jesus' promise to the Good Thief, "*This day you will be with Me in Paradise.*"[5] Mary was recalling Jesus' Words of consolation to the whole world, for

---

[3]Mark 14:51
[4]Luke 23:34
[5]Luke 23:43

the whole world. Was it not important, when she missed her Son so very much, that Mother Mary *remember* the reason her Son died, that we would one day be with Him in Paradise, even those who ask forgiveness at the last moment? Was she not giving comfort to families of loved ones who have died and may be in need of mercy?

When you are questioning Mother Mary's role in the Redemption of the world, stop and ask yourself a question. How did St. Luke know so much about the suffering and death of our Lord Jesus Christ? There is no mention of St. Luke at the foot of the Cross. He had to have received his knowledge of Jesus' suffering on the Cross from Jesus' Mother. How much pain did our Blessed Mother endure for our sake, as she remembered her Son's pain, the pain of abandonment, of aloneness, of torture, and rejection? And for all, even those of us who still attack her Son.

"Father, into Your Hands, I commend My Spirit."[6] What had been your thoughts, Mother Mary at these words of your most beloved and precious Son? Were you relieved the suffering was over? Were you too deep in grief to rejoice that your Son would be reunited with His Heavenly Father? At first, there must have been solace that no one could hurt Him any longer, but as you had to dig up every painful step in His Walk to our salvation, and share them with St. Luke, were your wounds reopened? Did you ache to hold your Son in your arms, again, as you retraced His last Words?

And then, there are the Angels with Him at the Cross. They had been with Jesus from the Incarnation. They had shared that great moment when Heaven met earth and we were united with God. They had announced His Birth! Now, those He came for, those He had come to save, killed Him! We can envision the Angels crying hard tears and

---

[6]Luke 23:46

feeling justified anger as they watched the scandal of the Crucifixion unfold.

Mother Angelica tells us the only *justified anger* is *God's anger*. There have been many instances of God's Anger in the history of the world. We believe when Hitler massacred six million innocent Jews, Catholics and citizens, he incurred God's Anger, and when Stalin murdered ten million human beings, *he* aroused God's Anger, and as mothers world-wide are slaughtering their own flesh and blood, their helpless unborn babies, over thirty million in the United States alone, those who do (abortion) and those who do nothing invoke God's Anger.

But this, the murder of His only Son, Our God, we *truly* believe this was a time of God's Anger, and He allowed the Angels to manifest it for Him.

"My God, My God, why have You forsaken Me?" Did they cry out to Jesus, *"No, Lord, God your Father has not forsaken you! We have not forsaken You. It is those down there with You, those you came to save, they have forsaken You, Lord, not us. We love You. Give us one word, one sign and we'll make our slaughter of the 185,000 Assyrian soldiers who insulted You,*[7] *seem like child's play. Give us the nod, Lord, and we'll wipe out every one of them."*

As Jesus cried His last cry and painfully breathed His last breath, could it have been the screams of the Angels, horrified by the blasphemous act of our loving Savior's murder, that caused the curtain to be torn in the Temple from top to bottom, the earth to shake violently, the rocks to split, the sun to blacken, and the graves to open? Could that massive convulsion of the earth have been caused by the justified anger of God, as conveyed to us by His Angels?

But the Scandal of the Cross became the Triumph of the Cross!

---

[7] 2Kings 19:35

John's Gospel is unique. He dwells on different details than the other Gospel writers. *He was an eye-witness.* Our belief has always been that John regarded the end of Jesus' physical existence on this earth as the Triumph of the Cross, rather than the Scandal of the Cross. While the others in retrospect, may have understood and accepted the necessity of Our dear Lord Jesus having to suffer as much as He had, and in the manner He had, only John actually put it down on paper. He methodically tracked the incidents in the Crucifixion and Death of Our Lord Jesus and how they fulfilled Scripture, from Pilate's labeling Jesus "*King of the Jews*", and not giving in, insisting: "*What I have written, I have written.*" to the seamless tunic Jesus was wrapped in, woven in one piece from top to bottom, a sign of royalty or priesthood. It is also believed John referred to *Unity* in the tunic as the *unity* of the Church.[8]

St. Luke does not mention Mother Mary at the foot of the Cross because Mother Mary would not have wanted to bring attention to herself at the cost of keeping our eyes on Jesus. But John mentions Our Lady was at the foot of the Cross because it was John who was there with her, and it was important to him that the Faithful know the part *our* Mother had in our salvation.

"*When Jesus saw His Mother and the disciple there whom He loved, He said to His Mother, 'Woman, behold your son.' Then He said to the disciple, 'Behold your mother.' From that hour, the disciple took her into his home.*"[9]

The words highlighted are *Woman* and *hour*. The first time we hear Jesus calling His Mother "Woman" is at the Wedding Feast of Cana when "*Jesus said to her, 'Woman,*

---

[8]When we wrote our book "Scandal of the Cross and Its Triumph", little did we expect to write this book on the Rosary. In that book, the Lord told us to write how He grieves until we are one, and now His Word is the same - Unity!

[9]Jn 19:26-27

how does your concern affect me? My hour has not come yet."[10] and the last time is at Jesus' Final Hour. These words, *Woman and hour* appear when Jesus speaks to His Mother at the very beginning of His Ministry, and at the very end.

Mother Mary, as you went over every word your Son ever uttered, did you think about the time at Cana when you encouraged Jesus to change the water into wine? If you had not reached out to Him, that night, would He have died so horribly on the Cross? As you remembered Jesus' words at Cana did Jesus' last words on the Cross take on added pain?

At Cana Jesus tells us, as He says yes to His Mother and performs His first Miracle, that He will grant any petition, as long as it is the Father's Will, through His Mother's request. When Jesus gave Mother Mary to John, and John to Mother Mary, Jesus declared Mary the Mother of all Christians, *our* personal Heavenly Mother, and Mother of the Church.

Much is given to the fact that Jesus *first* gave John to His Mother, and *then* His Mother to the disciple. John represents us, the Church. Jesus gave the *Church* to His Mother *first*. He gave the Church over to her for her guidance and protection. She would care for us. Whenever we, the Church are in trouble and it seems the jaws of hell will finally do us in, Mother Mary comes in an apparition to affirm her Popes and to strengthen her Church.

When Jesus gave His Mother to John, He also gave Mother Mary to us as Mother of our Church, and our very own Mother. When we are disturbed by what we hear going on in the Church, do we turn to our Mother for help? The Church is her child. What mother, when her child is in danger, will not come forth to save him or her? Is this what Mother Mary has been saying, since Fatima? Is this part of

---

[10]Jn 2:4-5

the Third Secret of Fatima? Is Mother Mary grieving over the apostasy, division and dissension within the Church?

Jesus gave us His Mother as our *personal* Heavenly Mother, a Mother who would never forget us, who would be interceding for us, until the end of time. Are we listening with our heads and our hearts? Are we on our knees, turning to the Mother of God? When you think of the intense pain, Jesus had to go through to say these words, how can we doubt how important this was and is to Him? Jesus was suffocating! He had to summon every last vestige of strength to lift His pain-wracked Body, in order to say these words. It was that important. Jesus was, and is, putting us under the mantle and protection of His Mother.

When Jesus gave His Mother to John (as he stood in for us), was He not entrusting her to us? Was He not truly uniting us with Him, making us into family? Why do we not listen to the beautiful Mother He bequeathed to us? Turn to her! We fear this may be our last chance!

"....*aware that everything was now finished, in order that the scripture might be fulfilled, Jesus said, 'I thirst.' So they put a sponge soaked in wine on a sprig of hyssop and put it up to His mouth. When Jesus had taken the wine, he said, 'It is finished.' And bowing His head, He handed over His Spirit.*"[11]

When our Lord Jesus said "*I thirst.*" was it for all those who would never know Him and not knowing Him would not follow Him to His Father in Paradise? Was he thirsting for those souls? Was he thirsting over the millions of souls that would be lost because of the many false prophets that would rise up, over and over again in His Church, and lead so many of His innocent lambs astray?

John did not record Jesus' Human cries: "*My God, My God, why have You forsaken Me?*" Although this was plainly fulfillment of Psalm 22, we wonder if Jesus, in His pain was

---

[11]Jn 19:26-27

not even then thinking of us. Was He setting an example of the times we would cry out "*My God, My God, why have You forsaken Me?*" Was He, as our Brother, reaching out to us, telling us: "*It's all right. The Father and I forgive you. Wait until your Easter Sunday, your Resurrection. You'll see, We have not abandoned you. We have heard, and We have cried with you, just as the Father cried with Me in My pain and anguish. You are not alone. We are with you till the end of time!*"

We would like to try to reach into the hearts of the two Gospel writers who remembered and passed down our Lord's Words of anguish and abandonment. We believe that when Mark recorded Jesus' words to His Father, he was sharing also the pain St. Peter suffered the rest of his life because he had rejected his Jesus, the pain that made his martyrdom seem almost a relief. Mark is believed to have been St. Peter's secretary and we are sure *St. Peter, our first Pope*, shared many of his deepest feelings with him.

St. Matthew, our Gospel writer, was also one of the Apostles who had run away. We believe that he emphasized this part of the Passion because most likely he, too, mourned deeply not only our Lord's death, but the pain He suffered, as He struggled with His last words. Although it was painful recalling our Lord's Passion and death, and their part in it, these Gospel writers felt impelled to pass on His last moments and words.

But John was focusing on triumph, glory. This was the message of Jesus - the Good News! He did not want to blur the issue with anything that didn't lead in that direction.

With Jesus' last words "*It is finished*", the prophecies were completed; the price of salvation was paid; Redemption was accomplished. We became an Alleluia people, an Easter people; we were saved! We were saved by the Cross. And when Jesus said, "*It is finished*", He was saying the price has been paid; your redemption has been bought by the sacrifice of the Spotless Lamb; go and sin no more.

John continues unfolding the drama. It is not over for St. John. It is only beginning: "*But when they came to Jesus and saw that He was already dead, they did not break His legs, but one soldier thrust his lance into His side, and immediately blood and water flowed out.*"[12] The soldier was the centurion, Longinus, who then said, "*Surely, this was the Son of God.*"

[An aside, Longinus, who was partially blind, touched his eyes with the blood and water which flowed from the side of Jesus, and was immediately healed. He left the army, became a Christian, and evangelized in the area of Cappodocia until he was martyred for the Faith. He also came from the town that was renamed in honor of him, Lanciano (the Lance) where the oldest recorded Miracle of the Eucharist occurred.[13]]

This is an extremely important moment in the formation of the Church. We believe that the Church flowed forth from the Side of Christ in the form of His precious Blood and Water. The *Blood* represents the sacrifice of the Lamb for the world's salvation; and as the Church was formed at this moment, the salvation will come from the Church He formed - the Roman Catholic Church.

The *Water* is an outpouring of the Holy Spirit on the newly formed Church. The Lord said He would send down His Spirit, and send He did. So powerfully will the early Church be affected by this Spirit that in the first three hundred years, our Popes will have the Signal Grace to die as Martyrs, as will most of the Faithful.

Through His *Blood and Water*, we receive all the nourishment we need for our journey Home to the Father. We humans receive life-giving nutrients to all parts of our

---

[12]Jn 19:33-34

[13]Account in the book by Bob and Penny Lord's book: "*This is My Body, This is My Blood*, Miracles of the Eucharist."

bodies through the human blood that flows through our veins. And so, it is with our Church. This Blood that flowed from the Heart of Christ[14] continues to feed and strengthen the entire Body of Christ, through His Holy Eucharist. With the Water from His Side, we receive the *Living Water* that Jesus spoke of in Holy Scripture. As humans, we can not live without water. We can live without food for a period of time, but it is virtually impossible for a human to live indefinitely without water. And so, without His Living Water, our Church could not have lived on for 2000 years. From the side of Christ, from His most Sacred Heart, the infant Church was formed. And this Church exists today 2000 years later, and will exist until our Lord returns.

John paints a picture of a little band, mostly brave women, standing at the foot of the Cross. They represent the Church, faithful, sharing in the suffering and redemption of the Savior's Cross. They are the Church Triumphant, the Church that stands by our Lord, faithful to His Word and to His mandate: "*Do you really love Me? Feed My Lambs.*" As with the weeping women at the foot of the Cross, our Church mourns over one soul lost to the Lord and His Church, and rejoices when they return.

Archbishop Sheen tells us, "*It's not weakness to hang on the Cross; it's obedience to the law of Sacrifice. If He came down, He never would have saved us. It's human to come down off the cross; it's Divine to hang there.*" As we go on to embrace the rewards of the Crucifixion, the Resurrection, we must never forget the Passion of Our Lord Jesus Christ. We dare not bypass the Crucifixion, and go directly to the Resurrection. We cannot forget what Our Lord suffered to bring us to Redemption. We cannot belittle the sacrifice, the Son of God made for us.

---

[14]Because of the mixture of Blood and Water flowing from the Side of Christ, scientists say that the tip of Jesus' Heart had to have been pierced by the Lance.

More and more, our Protestant brothers and sisters are embracing Christ's suffering on the Cross. The offspring of the 6,000,000 children who had been lost to Protestantism are returning home to Mother Church. And we rejoice. The splinters of the Cross that were shattered by disobedience and misunderstanding are becoming whole once more, as brothers and sisters of Christ are coming back. And when they all return, then the *Scandal of the Cross* will truly become the *Triumph of the Cross*. The mourning of Good Friday and this Fifth Sorrowful Mystery will become the Alleluia of Easter Sunday and the First Glorious Mystery.

Our Lord said, *"Peace I leave with you. My Peace I give to you. Not as the world gives, do I give it to you."*[15] As you walk with Jesus and Mary through this Rosary, take Lent and Easter, Pentecost and Christmas into your heart. Relive the life of Jesus and Mary. Go into Holy Scripture. Get to know your Father in Heaven, His only begotten Son Jesus, the Holy Spirit, our Mother Mary, the Angels and the Church. Don't take any of it for granted.

Make each Mass, a reenactment of the Life, Death and Resurrection of Jesus Christ. Be for Jesus with every step you take, with every breath, with every beat of your heart. Walk the Way of the Cross on Friday nights not only during Lent, but every Friday evening. Spend time with Jesus in the Blessed Sacrament. Jesus suffered a heavy price so that we could have Him with us always.

Defend your Church against those who would compromise it, belittle it, or destroy it. And the best way to do that is by the way we actively, zealously love our Lord Jesus, and our brothers and sisters. Go to Him. He's waiting for you. Then see what graces will be bestowed upon your family, the Church, our country, the world by our Lord Who will not be surpassed in generosity.

---

[15]John 14:27

The Resurrection

Jesus said, "*The Son of Man must suffer greatly and be rejected by the elders, the chief priests and the scribes, and be killed, and on the third day be raised.*"[1] It was Sunday, the third day, but everyone had forgotten what He said about *the third day*, or didn't understand it.

Dawn was approaching. Most of the citizens of Jerusalem were sleeping, tired from the celebration of Passover, which had taken place the day before. Many of them had celebrated hard. They wanted to get the image of Jesus and the events of Friday out of their minds. Some had succeeded in forgetting the entire incident, by now. After all, it had happened two days ago. It was like yesterday's newspaper. Much had taken place in their everyday lives, since then. Besides, there were always plenty of self-styled prophets coming down the pike. There would be others.

But there were those who had not forgotten, those who wanted to go to the tomb to give the Master a proper burial. When Jesus was taken down from the Cross, it was too late to prepare His Body for burial, as sundown was quickly approaching. It was Friday, the beginning of the Jewish Sabbath. According to the Law, they would have to wait until after the Sabbath (sundown Saturday). Joseph of Arimathea stepped forward and offered the tomb, he had bought for himself. They placed the Lord's Body in the tomb. But it was a hurried affair.

Now the Sabbath was over. Three women headed for the tomb. They were Mary Magdalene, Mary, mother of James and John, and Salome. They brought perfumed oils to anoint the Body; they would now *properly* give honor to their Lord Jesus. They wondered about the huge stone

---

[1]Luke 9:22

which had been placed in front of the tomb. How would they move it? It was too heavy for the three of them. Maybe the soldiers would still be there. Would they help? That was a toss-up. But they would have faith; God would get the stone removed. All they needed was to trust.

At this end of the spectrum, the women were heading towards the tomb; and at the other end, curtains separating Heaven and earth, were splitting open. A fiery Angel was swooping towards earth. He was brilliant. He was powerful. We read in the Gospel of St. Matthew,

"And behold there was a great earthquake. For an Angel of the Lord descending from Heaven, and coming, rolled back the stone, and sat upon it. And his countenance was as lightning and his raiment as snow. And for fear of him, the guards were struck with terror, and became as dead men."[2]

Our Lady didn't go with the other three to the tomb. She had been with them the whole weekend, but when they wanted to leave early on Sunday morning to head for the tomb, she stayed behind. She had no need to go. She knew her Son was not there. She remembered what everyone else had forgotten, or never understood: *Jesus had predicted His Resurrection*!

"Taking the twelve aside, He said to them: 'We must now go up to Jerusalem so that all that was written by the prophets concerning the Son of Man may be accomplished. He will be delivered up to the Gentiles. He will be mocked and outraged and spat upon. They will scourge Him and put Him to death, and on the third day, He will rise again.' They knew nothing of this. His utterance remained obscure to them, and they did not grasp His meaning."[3]

---

[2]Matt 28:2-4
[3]Luke 18:31-33

Although the others did not understand, Mary *did* understand what her Son was telling her, and us. She knew and she believed. She had no reason to doubt. While it's not in Scripture, our Tradition tells us that the first person Our Lord Jesus would have come to was His beloved Mother. It makes sense. She was the closest human being to Him. Why not Mary?

Mother Mary had suffered painfully during the Passion and Death of Our Lord Jesus. It was as if someone had ripped her heart out of her body. [I remember when our son died, I felt as if my heart was bleeding.] It hadn't mattered that Mother Mary knew that He was the Son of God, and that He would rise from the dead. Her cross, the horror of witnessing what had been done to her Son was more than a Mother should have to bear. *That was her Baby they beat and spit at!* That was the Boy she had held on her lap. And now, they were hanging Him on a cross. She had stood alone beneath that cross with only St. John and the ladies there to console her.

When they lowered our dear Lord into her arms, St. John and the other women stood a respectable distance. They gave Mary a private moment with her Son, as she said good-by, one last time. They had stood by Mary to the very end. Now, she would set aside her pain and offer *them* hope and consolation. After Our Lord Jesus was placed in the tomb, Mother Mary left for the Upper Room. She wanted to comfort St. John and the ladies, as they had comforted her in her time of grief.

The Apostle's Creed tells us "*He descended into Hell...*" We believe by this, Our Lord Jesus went into the Limbo of the Fathers,[4] where He freed the early Fathers of the

---

[4]Catholic Encyclopedia - James Broderick - That state or reserve in which the souls of the just, such as Abraham, Isaac and Jacob, were detained until the complete redemption by Christ through which Heaven was opened to them.

Church.[5] He then returned to earth to be resurrected with His Body.   He brought with Him all the holy Fathers, actually, everyone whom He had released from Limbo. They all went with Jesus to the tomb, where His beaten and bruised Body lay in wait. They all beheld the price, He had paid for the ransom of their souls, and ours.[6]

†

Then, His soul was united with His Body. There was such a burst of light, such a massive release of energy which united the Body of the Savior with His Soul, that upon impact, a blinding, jarring intensity took place which caused His Image to be projected onto the Shroud in an image[7] not unlike that of a negative. After this great explosion of light, the Glorified Body of Our Lord Jesus rose from the tomb.

"It is an ancient Tradition of the Church that Jesus appeared first to His Mother in solitude. It could not have been otherwise, because she is the first and principal co-redeemer of the human race, in perfect union with her Son."[8]

We believe that Our Lord went to His Mother first. At the moment of Resurrection, Our Lady felt the overpowering presence of her Son. She always knew when He was in her presence. But it was different this time. Now, He had come back from the dead! She could feel the *Divinity* of her Son, His radiance, His aura, roaring through her. She turned to see Him standing beside her, looking at her with so much love. Whereas she always believed the

---

[5]According to the writings of Venerable Sister Mary Agreda in her book - City of God

[6]City of God - Sr. Mary Agreda

[7]In Hiroshima, in 1945, when the Atomic bomb exploded, images of people on the street were projected onto the side of a building from the sheer light-force of the impact.

[8]Conversations with God: Book 2 - Francis Fernandez

words of the Angel, that she was the Mother of God,[9] this may possibly have been the first time she actually experienced Him in His glorified state. She *knew* she was in the presence of God.

She prostrated herself before the Resurrected Jesus. He lifted her up, and brought her close to Him. There was an infusion of His light and aura which flowed into her. In a sense, they returned to the intimacy they had enjoyed when He was in her womb. Only now, rather than Mary's blood flowing into her unborn Baby, the Power of Heaven, the strength to go on, was flowing through her from her Son, the God-Man, now more God than Man. She experienced an opening of her senses. She received wisdom and knowledge, discernment and joy, unlike anything she had never known. She was given the gift of Heaven on earth.

"The gospels do not tell us of the appearance of the risen Christ to Mary. Nevertheless, since she was specially close to the Cross of her Son, she must also have had a privileged experience of His Resurrection."[10]

She remained in His presence as long as He was there. She would never have left Him, but she knew that, like when He was on earth, He still had much to do. She spoke to all the early Fathers of the Church, now called Saints of the Church, including her dead husband St. Joseph, and her mother and father. She humbly prostrated herself before them, even though she was of a much higher station. We believe that seeing her Son and loved ones in their heavenly state gave Mother Mary the strength to say yes one more time - only now it would be to the pain of life on earth without her Son. When Jesus left her, she prayed quietly, savoring this special moment in her heart. It would have to last her for close to twenty long years.

---

[9]Luke 30-32
[10]John Paul II - Homily, 31 January 1985

†

When Mary Magdalene, Mary the mother of James and John, and Salome arrived at the tomb, the stone had already been rolled back. There was quiet all around. They peered in. It was empty. Again, we go to the Gospel of St. Matthew.

"And the Angel said to the women: 'Fear not, for I know that you seek Jesus, Who was crucified. He is not here, for He is risen, as He said. Come and see the place where the Lord was laid. Go quickly, tell all His disciples that He is risen, and behold, He will go before you into Galilee, there you shall see Him.'"[11]

Mary Magdalene and the other two women ran back to the Upper Room, as quickly as they could. They were completely out of breath, when they arrived. Mary Magdalene spoke first to Peter and John. She recounted to them what the Angel had said. The Apostles and disciples didn't believe any of it. But Peter and John *immediately* ran to the tomb. It was still very early in the morning. When they arrived, the soldiers were not to be seen anywhere. They went to the tomb, and peered inside. It was as the women had told them, only there was no Angel in attendance. John went inside the tomb. He believed. Peter, on the other hand, went home *amazed* at what he had seen.[12]

Mary Magdalene returned to the tomb. She looked around, not really knowing what she was trying to find. She saw two Angels sitting inside the tomb. They spoke to her. *"Woman, why are you weeping?"* She responded, *"Because the Lord has been taken away and I do not know where they have put Him."*[13] She sensed the presence of someone behind her. She turned around and saw Jesus, but she did not recognize

---

[11]Matt 28:5
[12]Luke 24:12
[13]John 20:13

Him. He repeated the question, the Angels had asked her. *"Woman, why are you weeping? Who is it you are looking for?"*

She was in a frenzy. She didn't want to engage in conversation. She wanted to find Jesus! She pleaded with the Man, trying to control herself, as she was a little out of sorts, *"Sir, if you are the one who carried Him off, tell me where you have Laid Him, and I will take Him away."*[14] It only took one word from Jesus to open the eyes of Mary. He called to her, so tenderly, *"Mary"*. She immediately recognized that it was He, her Master, her God. She reached for Him, crying out *"Rabboni"*, which means *Teacher*. He cautioned her,

"Do not cling to Me, for I have not yet ascended to the Father. Rather, go to My brothers and tell them, 'I am ascending to My Father, and your Father, to My God and your God.'"[15]

Now, she didn't care what anyone said. She had seen the Lord, and that was it. She went back to the disciples, and told them as much. But many of them still could not bring themselves to believe.

The Upper Room

As evening began to close that day, the Apostles (all except Thomas) and many of the disciples, were gathered at the Upper Room. They were frightened; they felt lost; they had no place to go. They locked and barred the doors securely. There had been rumors that Jesus' followers had stolen the Body from the tomb, and were claiming that He had risen from the dead. The Apostles and the disciples stood huddled in fear that the Jews would be looking for them, to blame *them*. Now Jesus' followers had also heard that Jesus had risen, but most of them didn't believe it; they discounted it as idle gossip. It was so hard for the Lord's own people to believe in Him. How difficult would it be to

---

[14]John 20:15
[15]John 20:15-17

get the whole world to believe? What would it take? We go to Holy Scripture:

"Abraham said to him (the rich man), 'If they do not listen to Moses and the prophets, they will not be convinced even if one should rise from the dead.'"[16]

Jesus knew they were a hard lot to convince, even His own Apostles and disciples did not have the faith to believe. He would do whatever it took. So that evening, as they were all sitting together, cringing, bemoaning their situation, Jesus came *through* locked and bolted doors and sat among them. He convinced them He was not merely a Spirit, but Body and Spirit; He asked for food, and *ate* it in their presence. They were all excited once more.

He blessed them. He said to them, *"Peace be with you."* Then He commissioned the eleven to be Apostles. He said to them, *"As the Father has sent Me, so I send you."*[17] The meaning of Apostle is *"those sent"*. By this statement of Jesus, he was commissioning them and us through them, to go out and spread the Good News.

And then, knowing that man cannot receive the Good News, no less be healed physically, with crippling sin on his soul, Jesus gave them the mandate to forgive sins. Our Lord gave us here, through the Apostles, the *Sacrament of Reconciliation,* or Penance, the forgiveness of sins. He breathed on them and said,

"Receive the Holy Spirit.
If you forgive men's sins,
they are forgiven them;
if you hold them bound,
they are held bound."[18]

---

[16]Luke 16:31
[17]John 20:21
[18]John 20:23

Monumental events took place at this first meeting, after His Resurrection, between Jesus and His Apostles. *He breathed the Holy Spirit on them.* By this, he was breathing new life into them. It was a foreshadowing of the Descent of the Holy Spirit, which would take place on Pentecost Sunday. But it was at this very first meeting, after His Resurrection, that He also gave them His mandate to go out and evangelize under the inspiration of the Holy Spirit. Holy Scripture is very clear on this point. And then, Jesus gave The Apostles, and those who would follow, the power to forgive sins.[19]

The Road to Emmaus

If that was not enough, He gave us another *powerful* sign, when He appeared to the disciples on the Road to Emmaus;[20] He affirmed the Holy Eucharist.

To paraphrase the Gospel, two disciples were on the Road to Emmaus. They were completely distraught. It was all over, they thought. With the death of Jesus, all the hope of the new covenant was lost. They were sharing their distress when a stranger began to walk with them. He seemed to be unaware of all that had happened. The disciples said to him, *"You must be the only citizen in Jerusalem who doesn't know about the events of this past week-end."* Then they proceeded to share how they believed Jesus to be the Messiah, the Anointed one, and how the chief priests and elders killed Him, crucifying Him like a common criminal.

The Stranger spoke to them. *"O foolish and slow of heart to believe in all things which the prophets have spoken. Ought not the Christ to have suffered these things, and so to enter into His Glory?"*[21] He went from scripture passage to

---

[19]This was confirmed by the Council of Trent
[20]Luke 24:13-32
[21]Luke 24:25-26

scripture passage, affirming everything that had happened, how the Son of Man *had to undergo* the Passion and die that Scripture would be fulfilled. The disciples found themselves coming out of their depression. As He spoke, understanding and hope cut through the cloud of darkness they had felt. Their hearts were pounding with the Spirit as they listened, spellbound, to the Stranger.

When they got to Emmaus, the Stranger continued on, as if He were going farther. The disciples stopped Him. *"Don't leave us!"* they said. *"It's getting late. Stay with us."* [Can you imagine being in the presence of the Lord and Him speaking to you? Do you spend quiet time before the Blessed Sacrament? He's there and if you will only be silent, He will talk to your heart.]

The Stranger stayed with them. They all sat at table. He took bread, blessed it, broke it, gave it to them, and their eyes were opened. They saw that it was Jesus. With that, He disappeared from their sight. They rushed back to Jerusalem to tell the Apostles and disciples what had happened. On their way, they marveled to each other, *"Didn't our hearts burn as he spoke to us on the road and explained Scripture to us?"* Their hearts burned with the Word, but they recognized Him in the breaking of the bread.

Doubting Thomas

In John's Gospel, we learn that Thomas was not with the other Apostles when Jesus appeared to them on Easter Sunday. When they told him all that had transpired, he refused to believe them, making the famous statement: *"Unless I see the marks of the nails in His Hands, and put my fingers into the nail marks, and put my hand into His side, I will not believe."*[22]

How many of us are, or have been at any given time in our lives, Doubting Thomases, or Doubting Thomasitas?

---

[22]John 20:24-29

The following week, Our Lord Jesus appeared to the Apostles, again, in the Upper Room. This time Thomas was with them. Jesus came through the bolted, locked door. He directed Himself immediately to Thomas: *"Put your fingers here and see My hands, and bring your hand and put it into My side, and do not be unbelieving, but believe."*[23]

In the form of an apology, and also a proclamation of his belief, Thomas said to Jesus, *"My Lord and my God"*. Now something very important happened here. Jesus would not let Thomas off with his apology. Believing in the Lord was much too important to let it go with a slap on the wrist. The Lord continued, *"Have you come to believe because you have seen Me? Blessed are those who have not seen and believe."*[24]

Do we believe in Him? Or are we Doubting Thomases? Do we have to have it proven to us, like Thomas? Will we believe even then; or are we those, the Lord referred to in the parable of the dead Rich man:

"Once there was a rich man who dressed in purple and linen and feasted splendidly every day. At his gate lay a beggar named Lazarus who was covered with sores. Lazarus longed to eat the scraps that fell from the rich man's table. The dogs even came and licked his sores. Eventually the beggar died. He was carried by the Angels to the bosom of Abraham. The rich man likewise died and was buried. From the abode of the dead, where he was in torment, he raised his eyes and saw Abraham afar off and Lazarus resting in his bosom.

"He called out, 'Father Abraham, have pity on me. Send Lazarus to dip the tip of his finger in water to refresh my tongue, for I am tortured in these flames.' 'My child,' replied Abraham, 'remember that you were well off in your lifetime, while Lazarus was in misery. Now he has found consolation here, but you

---

[23]John 20:27
[24]John 20:29

have found torment. And that is not all. Between you and us, there is a great abyss, so that those who might wish to cross from here to you cannot do so, nor can anyone cross from your side to us.'

"'Father, I ask you, then,' the rich man said, 'send him to my father's house where I have five brothers. Let him be a warning to them so that they may not end in this place of torment.' Abraham answered, 'They have Moses and the prophets. Let them hear them.' 'No, Father Abraham,' replied the rich man. 'But if someone would only go to them from the dead, then they would repent.' Abraham said to him, 'If they do not listen to the prophets, they will not be convinced even if one should rise from the dead."*[25]

Jesus is speaking to them and to us, today. Do we believe or are we those of whom Jesus is speaking? "*Even if a man returns from the dead, they will not believe.*" Is Jesus crying out to us, will there be any faith here on earth when He returns? "*But when the Son of Man comes, will He find faith on earth?*"[26]

Jesus knew and knows that in the coming centuries, more people would *not* see Him than would see Him. They had to believe! How would they believe? We go to John's Gospel: "**I pray not only for them, but for those who will believe in Me through their word.**"[27] The answer is, through us. We have to do the job. As Mary said to Juan Diego, when she appeared as Our Lady of Guadalupe:

"*Listen well my son, and understand. I have many messengers I could send, and any one of them would be accepted immediately. But it has to be you!*"

We don't have the luxury of waiting for a personal appearance by Jesus or Mary. We don't have the time to go all over the world researching or authenticating visions or

---

[25]Luke 16:19-31
[26]Luke 18:8
[27]John 17:20

visionaries. There's too much work to be done. We have our churches, and the Blessed Sacrament in each of these churches. This is why Jesus left Himself to us in His Holy Eucharist, in His Holy Church. What does Jesus want of us? We must listen and believe what He tells us, in His Word, taking it in our head, and acting through our heart.

St. Paul asks the question: *"And how can they believe in Him of whom they have not heard? And how can they hear without someone to preach? And how can people preach unless they are sent? As it is written 'How beautiful are the feet of those who bring Good News!'"*[28]

Our dear Lord Jesus loves us so much, He never stops trying to help us. We see, even after His death, how He continues to come back to us to give us strength, to give us courage, to give us power. He gives us His Body, through the Eucharist, His Mother, through the Rosary, His Church through His Vicar, our Pope John Paul II. He believes in us. He has faith in us. He sees something in us that we surely don't see in ourselves. We can't see the beauty He envisioned in us from the beginning of Creation.

Allow Jesus to be resurrected in your heart, in your soul. Allow His Holy Spirit to enter into you, and fill you with such strength and such power, that you will change the world before it's too late. Allow the Mother of God to guide you and direct you in the path Jesus and the Father have laid out for you. Listen to the Angels when they speak to you. They're here to bring you through the narrow gate to your own Resurrection. Praise Jesus.

---

[28]Romans 10:14-15

The Ascension

Scripture tells us that Jesus appeared to His disciples many times between His Resurrection and His Ascension into Heaven.[1] The second time He appeared to His Apostles after His Resurrection, which is *recorded* in Scripture, was on the Sea of Galilee.[2]

Jesus had told Mary Magdalene to tell the brothers that He would see them in Galilee. To that end, they went up to Galilee, to the Sea of Galilee. They became restless, waiting for Jesus. Or was it they just decided to take part in something very familiar to them, fishing? There is safety in doing. You don't have to think! But the life they had had with the Master would not remain buried. How many memories there must have been, as they prepared their nets, and cast out to sea. How many important events had taken place on the Sea of Galilee! The Ministry of Jesus began on the Sea of Galilee. He preached on the sea, on Peter's boat. Peter and Andrew, James and John, had been chosen *here*. The Lord had given them the great catch of fish on this Sea. *Here*, He had told them they were to be *fishers of men*. Jesus walked on water and calmed the storm, on this sea. So many memories! What was their future to be, they wondered. Perhaps they even shared on it. Was it over? Did Jesus have more for them to do? What was the plan?

This day, as they cast out to sea, there was almost a replay of the first time Peter had encountered Jesus.

†

The first time, there were *crowds* listening to Jesus teaching the Word of God by the Lake of Gennesaret. Jesus caught sight of two boats close to the bank. He got into one

---

[1] John 20:30 - *"Now, Jesus did many other signs in the presence of His disciples which are not recorded in this book."*

[2] John 21:1-25

of the boats (Simon Peter's) and asked him to put out a little from the shore. Then Jesus sat down in the boat and began to teach. When Jesus finished teaching, He told Peter to *"put out into deep water and cast out your nets for a catch."* [Simon Peter remembered it like it was yesterday.] Simon Peter told Jesus that they had been fishing all night and had caught nothing; but if He said so they would cast out their nets. The amount of fish caught was so great, they thought they would break their nets.[3]

†

Now, here was Simon Peter and the disciples, three years later, once again by the shore. They had been fishing all night and had caught nothing. It was early morning when they spotted a Man on the shore. He called out to them; He suggested they cast off in a different place. Peter looked towards the shore. It didn't look like Jesus, and it didn't sound like Jesus. But something about the situation was reminding Him of the first time they had met Jesus. They did as the Man told them. The results were the same, this time, as they had been the first time. Their nets were heavy with fish. Then John whispered to Simon Peter, *"It is the Lord!"* Simon Peter excitedly jumped out of the boat and swam for shore. Meanwhile, the others brought the boats in with their great catch. As they approached the shore, they saw flames rising from smoking charcoals, inviting them to come closer.

Jesus told them to bring to Him some of the fish they had caught. He then proceeded to cook them breakfast. They did not recognize Him as *Jesus*, but they *knew* it was He. *They just knew.* They all sat around Him, as He fed them. It was so good to be in the presence of the Lord again. One moment, they were filled with peace, and the next moment they were so excited they could hardly contain

---

[3]Luke 5:4-6

themselves. They felt as if their hearts would burst from happiness. It was not over; it was as He had said. They would go on; the ministry would continue. They were so very much on fire. They had new strength; He was with them. All was well with the world. They were happy they were eating, we're sure, but the physical feeding was not as important to them as the spiritual feeding, and their joy that the Master was with them, and would never leave them.

After breakfast, Jesus spoke to Peter. *"Simon, son of John, do you love Me more than these?"* Peter answered without hesitation, *"Yes, Lord, You know that I love You."* Jesus commanded him, *"Feed My lambs."*

Jesus asked Peter a second time, *"Simon, son of John, do you love Me?"* Peter answered again, *"Yes, Lord, You know that I love You."* Jesus said, *"Feed My sheep."*

Again, Jesus asked Peter, *"Simon, son of John, do you love Me?"* Peter was hurt that Jesus had asked him again, 'Do you love Me?' He answered *"Lord, You know everything; You know that I love You."* Jesus commanded him again, *"Feed my sheep."*[4]

There is much we can gather through this conversation of Our Lord Jesus with Peter. What comes to mind immediately is Peter's denial of Jesus. Three times on Holy Thursday evening, Peter denied he even knew Jesus. At the Last Supper, Jesus had predicted he would do that. Was Jesus reminding Peter of what he had done? Was He letting Peter know He hadn't forgotten, even though He had never mentioned it again? Was He telling Peter that, as head of the Church, he could never ever do that again, or even entertain the thought? Or was Jesus saying, He was wiping clean the slate, each time Peter said he loved Him, and said yes to showing that love, by feeding the Lord's sheep (that's us)? Could that be why Jesus asked Peter three times if he

---

[4]John 21:15-17

loved Him, to cancel out Peter's three denials? Why not?
Peter was being forgiven by his profession of love and his
yes! Peter had denied Jesus three times. Now Jesus was
asking him to put that away for all time by proclaiming his
love for Him, by accepting His mission for him: *"Do you love
me? Feed My sheep!"* Was Jesus not saying: "Whenever you
feed My sheep, you show your love for me. I am entrusting
you with them, Peter."?

Was Jesus saying that Peter was forgiven because he
was truly sorry? Did Jesus want him to know that He
forgave him *all*, and that as He had forgiven Peter, He knew
Peter would forgive others? Was Jesus telling Peter to
remember how he had known fear and He had shown mercy
on him? Now, he would show compassion on other
members of Christ's body who fell and needed a helping
hand getting up; because he was being made strong out of
his weakness.

As He spoke to Peter, Our Lord Jesus Christ was also
fulfilling His promise: "Upon this rock I *will* build My
Church. To you I *will* give the keys to the Kingdom of
Heaven" and now "Feed My sheep, feed My lambs." This is
not only the fulfillment of Christ's promise, but it is His
actual *commission* to Peter to take charge of the Church as
the vicar of Christ. As the sheep are Christ's sheep, (He says
plainly *My* sheep), Peter is a vicar, standing in for the Owner
Who is Jesus Christ. And all the Peters to follow, right up to
our Pope John Paul II are standing in for our Christ as they
feed Christ's sheep, we the Church.

†

How many times have we denied Jesus, perhaps not in
such dramatic ways as our first Pope, St. Peter, but in our
own ways? When we were younger, and wanted acceptance
by our friends, who may not necessarily have been Catholic,
or even Christian for that matter, were we willing to deny

Jesus for our friends? Did we deny Him by our silence, never letting on that we were Catholic, knowing this would make us unpopular? Oh, we never spoke out against Him, necessarily, but when someone used His name in vain, did we ask them to stop? When someone criticized the respect and importance we give to Mother Mary, did we defend her, reminding them that it was Jesus Himself Who gave Mary to us as our Mother and we were to revere her as His Mother and our Mother? Or did we do the popular thing and say nothing?

And as we got a little older, and we were being pressured to be part of situations that we were not comfortable with, but were socially acceptable, did we distance ourselves from anything that had to do with our soul and opt for acceptance? That's a form of denying Jesus.

In our business life, and married life, do we live a double standard? *Do what I say, but not what I do*? Do we treat our children that way? Is behavior acceptable for us because we're adults, while it's not for our children? Is drug abuse okay for us, in the form of smoking and drinking alcohol, while it's not okay for our children in other forms? Do we deny Jesus in that way? Do we even give it a second thought?

†

Our Church tells us that this passage was also an affirmation of Peter's role as head of the Church, or re-affirmation, or *final confirmation*. There would never be a question again about who was to lead the early Church. God had chosen Peter; it had been confirmed to Jesus, when Peter said to Jesus, *"You are the Messiah, the Son of the Living God."* Jesus knew this had not come from Peter. He couldn't possibly have thought of this on his own. Jesus replied, *"Blessed are you Simon, son of Jonah, for flesh and blood has not revealed this to you, but My Father. And so I say to you, you are Peter, and upon this rock, I will build My*

Church, and the gates of hell will not prevail against it. I will give you the Keys to the Kingdom. Whatever you bind on earth will be bound in Heaven; whatever you loose on earth will be loosed in Heaven."[5]

Nothing had changed from the time, Jesus proclaimed Peter as head of the Church, until this meeting. Peter had been chosen. That he had denied Jesus could have changed everything. But the fact that he had asked forgiveness sealed his role as head of the early Church. Jesus gives us a very clear picture of our Church, and the chain of command. By this announcement, Jesus told the world, loud and clear, that Peter and his successors are to hold the Keys to the Kingdom.

This was clarified when Jesus called His Apostles together for the last time. He brought them to Bethany, where He gave them final instructions. He said to them,

"All power in Heaven and on earth has been given to Me. Go, therefore, and make disciples of all nations, baptizing them in the name of the Father, and of the Son and of the Holy Spirit, teaching them to observe all that I have commanded you. And behold, I am with you always, until the end of the world."[6]

†

There's no question in our mind as to what Jesus was saying to us through our Fathers in Faith, the Apostles. We were given a clear mandate to Evangelize. We've heard the erroneous statement made, *"Catholics don't evangelize. We're the established Church of Jesus."* Take another look, my brothers and sisters. It's scriptural, folks. It's not optional. No one asked us if we had nothing better to do, if we weren't busy this weekend or next, perhaps we could spread the word of God. *"Power will be given you when the Holy Spirit*

---

[5]Matt 16:16-19
[6]Matt 28:18-20

comes." The Holy Spirit has come; He is here. *We do have Power.* We have to use it.

Very often, in our talks, we tell people they are *required* to evangelize, by our very Baptism into the Church. We tell the people about the unbalanced world situation we're looking forward to in the year 2,000. Statistically, there will be 6 billion people in the world, and 2/3 of that number, or 4 billion, will *never have heard the name of Jesus.* You know what our job is. We're commissioned, as the Apostles before us, to turn the tide, to give Jesus a birthday present in the year 2,000, of converts to the Faith, and a renewal of Faith from those who have not left.

Jesus also gave us security, strength, protection. He told the Apostles at that crucial time,

"And these signs will follow those that believe: in My Name, they shall cast out devils; they shall speak with foreign tongues. They shall pick up serpents, and if they drink any deadly thing, it will not harm them. They shall lay their hands upon the sick, and they shall recover."[7]

He further instructed them to stay in the city, *"And I send the promise of My Father (The Holy Spirit) upon you."*

John's Gospel instructed the Apostles in this way, *"But the Paraclete, the Holy Spirit, whom the Father will send in My name, will teach you all things, and bring all things to your mind, whatsoever I have said to you."*[8]

In Acts of the Apostles, we are taught *"....He enjoined them not to leave the city, 'but wait for the promise of My Father, about which you have heard Me speak, for John baptized with water, but in a few days, you will be baptized with the Holy Spirit.'"*[9]

---

[7]Mark 16:17-18
[8]John 14:26
[9]Acts 1:4-5

"....*you will receive power when the Holy Spirit comes upon you, and you will be My witnesses in Jerusalem, throughout Judea and Samaria, and to the ends of the earth.*"[10]

The Apostles must have thought Jesus was going to come back. They just stood there, waiting. They had heard what He said to them, but they didn't really understand. It would take the Descent of the Holy Spirit to open their minds to what Jesus was saying to them. It took the Angels to shake them out of their trance. They addressed the Apostles:

"*They still had their eyes fixed on the sky as He (Jesus) went away, when two men dressed in white suddenly stood beside them and said, 'Galileans, why are you standing there looking up at the sky? This Jesus, who was taken from you into Heaven, will come back in the same way that you saw Him go to Heaven.*'"[11]

The Apostles left the hill in Bethany, and made their way back to the Upper Room in Jerusalem. They were confused; their Master had left. He had given them instructions, most of which they understood; but His words, about the Holy Spirit coming, didn't sink in yet. This, they didn't understand. They had a great deal of faith in Jesus, however. Peter, who should be called Peter the Optimist, clung to the words of the Angels, "*This Jesus, who was taken from you into Heaven, will come back in the same way that you saw Him go to Heaven.*" He was filled with joy. He never thought to ask when or how Jesus was coming back. All that mattered was, He was coming back. Peter could wait. The Apostles left the hill, and went on their way, to begin the Church as we know it today.

Thus ended the life of Jesus on earth. It didn't end with the Crucifixion, but with His Ascension into Heaven.

---

[10]Acts 1:8
[11]Acts 1:10-11

And as the Angels were present for the Announcement of the Savior into the world, in the Annunciation to Mary, and in the proclamation to the shepherds in Bethlehem on that midnight clear, it was fitting that the Angels be there when His life on earth was ended.

Their job was not over by any means. While they would no longer be involved in His life on earth, they would definitely be involved in the Ministry of the Church, as messengers and intermediaries, and also in a very physical way[12] as protectors, in the lives of all the members of Christ's Church.

The Angels stood there, speaking to the Apostles, affirming what Jesus had said to them. The Angels watched the followers of Jesus leave. The Angels understood the words of Jesus. They knew what was going to happen on Pentecost Sunday. These dear men would be so filled with the Holy Spirit, there would be an explosion, catapulting the Apostles into leadership positions all over the world, proclaiming the Good News of the Kingdom. And the Angels knew that as the Kingdom of God spread to all the corners of the world, they would have their hands full, first protecting the Apostles, then their disciples, then the millions and billions of converts, us, for the next two thousand years, or more.

We praise You, Jesus for the gift of the Incarnation. We thank You, Lord, for the gift of the Resurrection, and Your Ascension into Heaven. We thank you for those Angels you left behind, to help us bring about Your Kingdom on earth.

---

[12]The Angels were very active in the lives of St. Peter (Acts 5:19-20)and Paul, (Acts 27:23-24) as well as other Apostles.

The Descent of the Holy Spirit

After the Resurrection of Our Lord Jesus, He stayed with His Apostles and Disciples for forty days to ingrain in them all the instruction He had given them regarding the Reign of God. As part of that teaching, He told them about the fulfillment of His Father's promise. They were about to return to Galilee. He told them not to leave Jerusalem. *"Wait, rather, for the fulfillment of My Father's promise, of which you have heard Me speak. John baptized with water, but within a few days, you will be baptized with the Holy Spirit."*[1]

He connected the Baptism of the Holy Spirit with the mandate for Evangelization. He said to them, *"You will receive power when the Holy Spirit comes down upon you; then you are to be my witnesses in Jerusalem, throughout Judea and Samaria, yes even to the ends of the earth."* With that, the Evangelist Luke tells us Jesus was *"lifted up before their eyes in a cloud which took Him from their sight."*[2]

From the very beginning, the gifts of the Holy Spirit were intended to give the followers of Jesus the fortitude and the power to fulfill the mandate to *evangelize.* That's why the gift was given them, this special *Signal Grace.* Jesus knew before He left them how much they would need it.

They really had no idea what Jesus meant. They were not ready for their transition from followers to leaders, from

---

[1]Acts 1:4-5
[2]Acts 1:9

fishermen to *Fishers of Men*, from lay people to Priests and Bishops and Popes. We're told that as He left them, they just kept looking up into the sky. They probably expected Him to come down again. But they were snapped out of their reverie by two Angels.

"*They were still gazing up into the heavens when two men dressed in white stood beside them. 'Men of Galilee,' they said, 'why do you stand here looking up at the skies? This Jesus Who has been taken from you will return, just as you saw Him go up into the heavens.'*"[3]

After the Ascension of our dear Lord Jesus, we have to believe that the big factor, that which gave them confidence to go back to the upper room, and wait and pray, was Mary. She was with them. She held them together. She was at the Ascension, and she went back with them and prayed with them for that first novena, that nine day period, knowing that if her Son said it, it would happen. She was their link with Jesus. If she stayed, for sure they were not dreaming; Jesus would send His Holy Spirit. They weren't quite sure what was going to happen when the Holy Spirit came. They knew they were supposed to go out to all the world, but how was that going to happen? They were fishermen. Jesus was the preacher; they were not. True, Peter had a big mouth; and John was a lovable person. Neither one was dynamic enough to have drawn a crowd on his own. But Mary was there. She lent credibility to everything. She made it right!

†

We were giving a talk at a CCD Conference. We made the statement: with our limited knowledge of the Saints (as there are thousands), we have never read of one who went directly to Jesus; they all went to Jesus through Mary.

---

[3]Acts 1:11

Well, this young man, a catechist, called me aside. He said, Bible tucked under his arm, ready for battle, "Well, I guess you don't know much about Holy Scripture." I conceded, probably not as much as he, but what was his problem? He said that the Apostles did not go through Mary, but went directly to Jesus. Now, he was playing in my court. Maybe I didn't know chapter and verse, but I knew the relationship between a mother and her child, between *the* Mother and her Son Jesus. Now, I was hot! "Are you telling me," I countered, "that our Lord Jesus was so cruel, He left His Mother behind for no reason?" If the Apostles and disciples did not need Mother Mary to represent her Son, to give them the strength and the courage to live for Christ and to later die for Him martyrs' deaths, why did Jesus not take her up with Him when He ascended? Why did He wait almost twenty years[4] to assume her into Heaven?

†

The Day of Pentecost and the Descent of the Holy Spirit

"When the day of Pentecost came, it found them gathered in one place. Suddenly from up in the sky there came a noise like a strong, driving wind which was heard all through the house where they were seated. Tongues as of fire appeared, which parted and came to rest on each of them. All were filled with the Holy Spirit. They began to express themselves in foreign tongues and make bold proclamations as the Spirit prompted them."(Acts 2:1-4)

The Apostles were so filled with the Holy Spirit, they began speaking in foreign tongues. They ran down, into the streets. Jews from different parts of the world were in Jerusalem that day. They heard the commotion. At first, they thought the Apostles were drunk. But then everybody could understand what they were saying, although all the

---

[4]according to City of God

Jews spoke different languages. Peter was on fire. He was the first to speak. He captivated them with his words and his zeal. He couldn't say anything wrong. On that day, Peter and the apostles baptized 3,000 people. From there it accelerated; it went on and on. Filled with the Holy Spirit, they followed Jesus' mandate, fulfilling His prophecy:

"You will receive power when the Holy Spirit comes down upon you; then you are to be my witnesses in Jerusalem, throughout Judea and Samaria, yes even to the ends of the earth."(Acts 1:8) Every day became a new Pentecost.

The rest of the Acts of the Apostles is dedicated to just that *one work* of the Apostles, their witnessing to the ends of the earth, in the name of the Father, and of the Son, and of the Holy Spirit. Fear and indecision had left them. *Power* surged through them. They went on to spend the rest of their lives as zealots in the service of the Lord. The Church as we know it today exists because of that explosion of *power* provided by the Holy Spirit. It was so strong it became contagious. The charismatic gifts of The Third Person of the Holy Trinity shot out from one to the other to the other, and on and on until disciples were running to the four corners of the earth, proclaiming the Good News of the Kingdom. Before you know it, Paul got into the picture. He carried the torch of the Holy Spirit into Asia, then to Europe, Greece, and *finally* to the center of the world of that time, Rome.

But the gift was not just for that time, or for those people. If it were for any time in the history of our Church, *it's for us, now!* We read it right there in Scripture. In that same chapter of Acts, where we read of the Descent of the Holy Spirit, in the very next section, *Peter's Discourse*, our first Pope addresses us, the Church of the final days, quoting from the Prophet Joel:

"It shall come to pass in the last days, says God,
that I will pour out a portion of my spirit
on all mankind;
Your sons and daughters shall prophesy,
your young men shall see visions
and your old men shall dream dreams.
I will work wonders in the heavens above
and signs on the earth below;
blood, fire, and a cloud of smoke.
The sun shall be turned to darkness
and the moon to blood
before the coming of that
great and glorious day of the Lord.
Then shall everyone be saved
who calls on the name of the Lord."[5]

St. Louis Marie de Montfort, one of Mary's heroes, a Marian prophet of the Seventeenth and Eighteenth centuries, and one of the most powerful advocates of Mary's place in the Church and in the world, had this to say about the role of the Holy Spirit through Our Lady in these last days.

"....towards the end of the world, ...Almighty God and His holy Mother are to raise up saints who will surpass in holiness most other saints as much as the cedars of Lebanon tower above little shrubs."[6]

"These great souls filled with grace and zeal will be chosen to oppose the enemies of God who are raging on all sides. They will be exceptionally devoted to the Blessed Virgin. Illumined by her light, strengthened by her spirit, supported by her arms, sheltered under her protection, they will fight with one hand and build with the other. With one hand they will give battle, overthrowing and crushing

---

[5]Acts 2:17-21
[6]True Devotion to Mary #47

heretics and their heresies, schismatics and their schisms, idolaters and their idolatries, sinners and their wickedness. With the other hand they will build the temple of the true Solomon and the mystical city of God, namely, the Blessed Virgin... "[7]

"They will be like thunder-clouds flying through the air at the slightest breath of the Holy Spirit. Attached to nothing, surprised at nothing, they will shower down the rain of God's word and of eternal life. They will thunder against sin; they will storm against the world; they will strike down the devil and his followers and for life and for death, they will pierce through and through with the two-edged sword of God's word all those against whom they are sent by Almighty God."[8]

"They will be true apostles of the latter times to whom the Lord of Hosts will give eloquence and strength to work wonders and carry off glorious spoils from His enemies. They will sleep without gold or silver and, more important still, without concern in the midst of other priests, ecclesiastics and clerics. Yet they will have the silver wings of the dove enabling them to go wherever the Holy Spirit calls them, filled as they are, with the resolve to seek the glory of God and the salvation of souls. Wherever they preach, they will leave behind them nothing but the gold of love, which is the fulfillment of the whole law.[9]

"They will have the two-edged sword of the Word of God in their mouths and the blood-stained standard of the Cross on their shoulders. They will carry the crucifix in their right hand and the rosary in their left, and the holy names of Jesus and Mary on their heart.[10]

---

[7]True Devotion to Mary #48
[8]True Devotion to Mary #57
[9]True Devotion to Mary #58
[10]True Devotion to Mary #59

"Mary scarcely appeared in the first coming of Christ... But in the second coming of Jesus Christ, Mary must be known and openly revealed by the Holy Spirit so that Jesus may be known, loved and served through her."[11]

†

Father Harold Cohen has been appealing to the people of God since we have known him, over six years, to ask to be filled with the Holy Spirit. He understands the value of the power of the Spirit. Now more than ever, he sees the need for us to have that *Power* on our side. The enemy has too much power. The ironic part of this is that we can have that *Power*. The scales can be balanced so easily. It's up to us. We all wail and moan that Satan is taking over the world, and that's true. But what nobody will come to terms with is, the reason that's happening is, we're allowing it. We're not taking advantage of that gift of the Descent of the Holy Spirit. That *strong driving wind, those tongues of fire, that fearlessness, that zealous nature* is ours for the asking. But we have to ask!

Our Lady said to us at the Chapel of the Miraculous Medal in Paris in 1830, *"But come to the foot of the altar. Great graces will be poured out on those who ask for them."* The key words here are, **"those who ask for them!"** When Catherine Labouré asked Mary why rays were not coming from all her fingers, she answered, *"These are graces which people have not asked for."*

Father Cohen tells us that when he was a child, his first words were not Mamma or Daddy; they were *"more"*. He still wants more, *more Holy Spirit*. We're not equating Father Cohen with St. Louis Marie de Montfort, *but then again, why not? We're all called to be Saints of these last days.* What about you? Are you a powerful saint of these last days? Ask for more. *Ask for the Holy Spirit!*

---

[11]True Devotion to Mary #49

The Assumption

Perhaps the greatest Fiat Our Lady had to make, was saying Yes to staying on earth after her Son Jesus had left her physically to prepare her place in Heaven. We must remember that she was with Him throughout His life, from the day He was born, through His early years, then His public ministry, to the day He was crucified. She had to have grieved terribly when He was taken from her.

We believe that when Our Lord Jesus rose from the dead, the first person He came to was His dear Mother Mary, even before appearing to the women at the tomb. If that is so, He may have given her the reason, at that time, why she had to stay on this earth. The only thing that makes sense would be for her to remain as a support system for the Apostles and disciples during these early days of the Church. Every time they looked at her, they would see Jesus. She was the living representative of Our Lord here on earth. They could draw strength from her.

But what a price He was asking her to pay. He had to know that her only desire was to be with Him. To stay on the earth while He left her was breaking a lifelong bond. Did Our Lord go to Mary and ask His most precious Mother to sacrifice precious time with Him, time when she could be with Him in Paradise, in order to nourish and protect the early Church? Was He entreating her to deprive herself of the Beatific Vision, for however long it would take for the Apostles to feel secure without her? If so, one thing we know; she said *Yes* again; because that always was, and still is, what Mary does; she says *yes*. But it had to be a very *hard* yes.

Our Lady went to Ephesus with John the Beloved for a time, and then she returned to Jerusalem. She could not have stayed away from the city where God had been so clearly present, by the physical presence of her Son, our Lord Jesus Christ. We're told she walked on the Via Dolorosa in Jerusalem every day, tracing and retracing the blood-stained footsteps of Jesus, as He walked to His death. We believe, with the price of her tears and pain, she remembered her Son's anguish on this Way of the Cross, and through Our Lady's actions, the Stations of the Cross, as we know them today, were instituted. Therefore, when you pray the Stations of the Cross, whether in your church or on Pilgrimage at a Shrine, or actually on the Via Dolorosa in Jerusalem, where it actually happened, you walk the Way of the Cross accompanied by the Mother who could not forget the Son Who walked the Way of the Cross. *Do this in memory of Him!*

†

"Come then, my love, my lovely one, come.[1]
"For see, winter is past, the rains are over, and gone."[2]
"Show me your face, let me hear your voice;
for your voice is sweet and your face is beautiful."[3]

†

It was time. Our Lady had remained on this earth too long. She wanted to see her Son again. She was tired. Little did she know that her Heavenly Family missed her as much, or perhaps even more than she missed them. The Angels and the Saints couldn't wait for their Queen, their Empress, to be brought into their midst. We're sure, Our Lord Jesus,

---

[1]Song of Songs 2:10
[2]Song of Songs 2:11
[3]Song of Songs 2:14

although He was always involved with matters of great consequence, missed His Mom also.

And so, let us attempt to see with our heart's eye what was going on in Heaven, and on earth. Our Lady was about to join Her Son in Heaven. We are sure her long time friend and princely consort, the Archangel Gabriel, was the one sent to earth to announce the Good News to Mary. She must have begun making preparations for her departure as soon as she heard. John was most likely the one she told. After all, he was the one who had been with her since Jesus died. We can see him breaking down in tears, at the thought of losing this most precious gem, but we know he understood and obeyed. As for her other children, the Apostles, our first Bishops, she told them without telling them. She tried to distance herself little by little. Could they sense she was preparing for a long trip?

It's three days before her dormition. We are in the Upper Room in Jerusalem. All the Apostles are expected at any time. We can just picture Peter and Paul being transported from Rome by Angels, as well as some of the others. Had the Angels informed them why they were being summoned to Jerusalem? They had known for some time that Mary's departure was imminent. Had they steeled themselves for it? No matter how hard we try, we cannot protect ourselves from the grief of separation. We can see these brave followers of Jesus breaking down like children, desperately trying to hold back tears in her presence, but not doing a very good job of it.

Our Lady was probably the most composed of the entire assemblage. She loved these children, as if they were her very own. They were her Son's community, the ones who were continuing His work on earth. They loved Him; they were loyal to Him. And she loved them, but she wanted to go Home. Her Son Jesus was waiting for her. On the day of her departure, she asked each of the Apostles to bless her, which they did. At this, they could not hold back any longer. They broke down completely, crying hard tears; they bent down and kissed the hem of her gown. They tried as best they could to capture a lasting memory of her breathtaking face in their *minds*, to burn the expression of her in their *hearts* for the rest of their lives.

Our Lady was not subject to the sins of Adam, having been immaculately conceived, born without sin. We believe she never aged beyond thirty-three years old (considered the perfect age), the age that Jesus died. While the Apostles and disciples watched their bodies break down and decay, she always remained that breathtakingly beautiful child/woman they had known from the day they had first met her. She never changed. But we are sure, she was tired. Could they not see that? We can see her blessing all the Apostles individually, as a great light filled the room. Jesus and His Angels had come to take His Mother home. Although they didn't see Him, we are sure they could feel His Presence. Was there a conversation between Jesus and Mary? She had waited for this moment. Our Lord beside her, she lay down, folded her hands, and went to sleep.

The Apostles stayed by her side for a long time, and then left the room. They decided that they would have the body of their Lady anointed with precious oils, the same as Our Lord Jesus' Body had been. They sent two of her maids into the room to do this. But the maids couldn't get near her body; the light was so brilliant, it blinded them. They left our Lady, and told Peter and John what had happened. They immediately ran into the room. The two Apostles knelt at the feet of their Queen. A voice from Heaven said she was not to be touched; Our Lord Jesus didn't want anyone undressing His Mother, not even her maids.

The Apostles could hear choirs of Angels singing. A unique fragrance of Heaven permeated the room. Her body and face glowed with a heavenly radiance. It was happening.

They knew it. She was being transported directly to Heaven by her Son Jesus and the Angels.

Is this the way it happened? We like to think so. Your conclusions are as good as ours. There have always been private revelations, but we are not required to believe them. Over the centuries, one thing has always been certain, in art and Tradition of our Church: Our Lord Jesus assumed His Mother, our sweet Mary, that perfect vessel, into Heaven, body and soul. To paraphrase our Pope Pius XII, *Jesus did it because it made sense to do it, and He had the power to do it.*[4]

There are many traditions as to when, and how, this all took place, such as where Our Lady's body may have been brought, to await her soul and her body uniting, as she was assumed into Heaven. Some say she was brought in procession to what is today called the Burial Place of Mary, at the Garden of Gethsemane, and placed in a tomb. They say, a huge stone was put outside her tomb, and guards stationed; three days later, her soul was united with her body, and she was assumed into Heaven, body and soul.

Another tradition is that her body was left in a chamber next to the Upper Room, where she had fallen asleep, and the Angels and Our Lord Jesus came for her there, and assumed her into Heaven. This room is now called Dormition Abbey (where Our Lady went to sleep), and is located right next to the Cenacle.

The tradition goes on to say that St. Thomas, *doubting Thomas*, was not there when she went to sleep. He came three days later, and wanted to venerate the body of his Queen. When he went into the room to pray before her body, he couldn't find her. She had already been assumed into Heaven. So naturally, *doubting Thomas* didn't believe. The tradition goes on to say that Our Lady appeared to Thomas, and verified that she had indeed been assumed into

---

[4]Munificentissimus Deus

Heaven, body and soul. And that he might believe, she removed the cincture, which she wore around her waist, and allowed it to float down from Heaven to St. Thomas. After that, he believed.

†

The tradition goes on to state that the cincture was brought to Italy by the Holy Crusaders during the first Crusade, and was placed in the Cathedral in Prato, Italy, where it can be found today. We went to the Church in Prato, to view the Heavenly Cincture. However, it takes three keys to open up the treasure. One is held by the Bishop, the other by the Custodian of the Cathedral, and the third, by the Mayor of Prato. It takes a great deal of coordination to be able to view the Cincture. Needless to say, we haven't seen the Cincture of Our Lady, yet!

These are all traditions, possibilities. Any and all are possible and probable. But none of that really matters. What we believe is that Our Lord Jesus did it, our Pope confirmed it, and that's enough for us.

†

"We pronounce, declare and define it to be a divinely revealed dogma: that the Immaculate Mother of God, the ever Virgin Mary having completed the course of her earthly life, was assumed body and soul to heavenly glory."

With these words, Pope Pius XII officially proclaimed the Assumption of Our Lady into Heaven, on the 1st of November in the Marian Year 1950, *the year of Mary*. The Dogma was called *Munificentissimus Deus*. On that day, what we Catholics had believed in faith, from the very beginning, was proclaimed authoritatively and *infallibly* by our Pope, who was a loving child of Mary.

The church's teaching on Papal infallibility applies to many statements, but the Papacy has only proclaimed it twice, making formal *ex cathedra* statements:

The first time was on December 8, 1854, when Pius IX declared the Dogma of the Immaculate Conception;

And *the second time* on November 1, 1950, when Pope Pius XII declared the Assumption of our Lady. The invocation "*Queen assumed into Heaven*" was added to the Litany of the Blessed Mother.

In this dogma, our Holy Father closed the door on speculation. He declared that any skepticism or unbelief in our Lady's Assumption, which may have been held throughout the years, was invalid. The Church assumed that such doubts were held in good faith, but that now, they can no longer be held. That's the exciting and reassuring thing about our Church. When the Pope declares it, we must believe it. That's it. There's no need for speculation, or indecision, *should I shouldn't I.* We just obey. The decision is taken out of our hands. God speaks through the successor to Peter, and, as the little girl/woman, whom we honor here did, we also say a simple, but resounding *yes.*

To quote our Pope Pius XII once more, "*Jesus did it because it made sense to do it, and He had the power to do it.*" There is so much logic to that statement. We're accused by our Protestant brothers and sisters of worshiping Mary. We don't worship Mary. But we do *love* Mary. We *venerate* Mary. We ask for her intercession with her Son. All this is so very natural. We would do the same with our earthly mother; why shouldn't we give this honor and respect to our Heavenly Mother? She is so very special in the eyes of the Lord. Why wouldn't He give her this honor? We thank You, Lord Jesus, for the gift of Your Mother. We know You have given her a special place in our lives, in the life of the Church. You said to John the Beloved, "*There is your Mother.*" You said to your dear Mother, "*There is your son.*" referring to us, the Church. Thank you for that gift, Lord Jesus. May we never take her for granted.

The Coronation

When we begin the Fifth Glorious Mystery, we use the title: *"The Coronation of Our Lady as Queen of Heaven and Earth, of all the Angels and the Saints."* As far as we can recall, we have always prayed this mystery under the title, "Queen of all the Angels and the Saints." But now that we think of it, we didn't really pray the Rosary much until we came back to the Church in 1975, and by that time, we were so in love with the Angels, and with their roles in our Church and our lives, we just naturally included them in this mystery.

This mystery is many things to us. It is Mary's reward for a life of humility, of submission and obedience, of *Fiat*. It's a definition of her role as Mother of the Church, and mediator between God and humanity. We don't really know how happy Mary's life on earth was. True, she was given a gift that no one in the history of mankind was given, that of bearing the Son of God in her womb, and living with Him for thirty three years. We don't know much about the years from twelve to thirty; it can be speculation or inspiration. And while the early days of His public ministry were glorious, full of excitement and achievement, miracles and healings, crusades and conversions, there was also the other side of the coin. There is always the other side of the coin.

There were those who hated Jesus, who called Him a fraud, a maniac, a devil. They were most likely more vehement in their condemnation of Jesus than those who were praising Him. There were the Pharisees and the Saducees, most of whom were against Jesus. Their protests against Him must have hurt Mary very deeply. We're sure these negatives didn't outweigh the positives, how God was being glorified through His Son on earth, but they were always there.

Possibly the worst, of the sorrows our Lady had to suffer, was the Passion and Death of our Lord Jesus. A beautiful man who had been a pall-bearer at our son's funeral, rushed away after the coffin was lowered into the ground. He called us at home. He apologized: "There is only one thing I can say and then I must hang up. There is an old Jewish expression, "*Parents should never have to bury their children.*" We witnessed the death of our son, who fell victim to an overdose of drugs. It was an outrage to watch this boy's life self-destruct before our very eyes. Our son died because he was a victim of the world and its false promises, its lies that we do not need to carry the Cross. With Mother Mary's Son Jesus it was different. Satan and his lies had no effect on Him.

He knew why He was born, and He said yes. He came to love us and to show us the love of God the Father. He came to show us the Face of God, to dispel the fear the Jews had always had of God, *that to see the Face of God was to die.* No longer would we fear to look upon Him. He came to bring us a touchable God, One Who laughed with us, cried with us, listened to us, walked with us. Jesus only wanted to love us. "*I have come to bring you life, and life more abundantly!*"[1] He *opened* up His arms to us, vulnerably, and

---

[1]John 10:10

we hung Him on a Cross. We killed Him. We killed her Son. Mary had to watch this, helplessly.

She may have known; she may have realized this was the Triumph of the Cross, not the Scandal of the Cross. She may have known; but she may not. And even if she did, this was her own Flesh and Blood who was being tortured and murdered before her eyes. He was God! But He chose *not to do anything,* but let it happen. He wouldn't even allow His Angels to defend Him.[2]   Mary understood.   But understanding is one thing, it's cerebral; feelings are something else, they are from the very depth of our being. We have to believe that although Mary may have *intellectually* known how her Son was fulfilling the Will of the Father, in her heart, in the pit of her stomach, she had to want to scream out for them to stop torturing her Son, stop hurting her little Baby.

Then there were the years after Jesus ascended into Heaven. She was here; He was there. Why did she have to stay on earth? Her work was over, wasn't it? Or was it? Did she have to continue to be Mother to all the Apostles and Disciples? Was she the living sign of Jesus in their midst, for the almost twenty years, she stayed here on earth?[3] Was this really necessary? Hadn't they received enough strength from the Holy Spirit, and the Angels who would be at their sides during the rest of their lives? No, they needed her presence here. She was the *Mother.* She had to continue to be Mother to the Apostles, to the disciples, to the entire Church for as long as Jesus wanted it.

We know Mary never made demands, and most probably she didn't expect any more than the honor which she was given to understand during her Magnificat. *"All generations shall call me blessed, for He who is mighty, has*

---

[2]Mat 26:53 - "Do you not suppose I can call on My Father to provide at a moment's notice more than twelve legions of Angels?"

[3]City of God, Sr. Mary Agreda

done great things for me, and Holy is His name."[4]   But considering all that she had suffered, plus the fact that *she had been chosen* to be the bearer of Jesus, the instrument, the Tabernacle, from which God would come forth, this final, ongoing tribute to her, was well deserved.   It was as if God the Father was saying to Mary and the whole world, "*This is My daughter, in whom I am well pleased.   Mary, thank you for your Yes!   Take your proper place in the Kingdom.*"

It's hard not to let your imagination run away with you, when you try to visualize in your mind's eye the pomp and ceremony, the great celebration of the Coronation of Mary as Queen of Heaven and earth, of all the Angels and the Saints. We know all the Angels had to be there. How many does that constitute?   Scripture tells us "*myriads upon myriads, thousands upon thousands.*"[5]

Consider, if you will, a great room.   That great room was a galaxy. The lineup of guests spread out as far as the horizon, in any direction.   In addition to the Angels, there were all the Saints, not just the ones we read about in the Lives of the Saints, but all those we don't read about, those we honor on November 1st, Feast of All Saints, those who were "*ransomed as the first fruits of mankind for God and the Lamb. On their lips no deceit has been found; they are indeed without flaw.*"[6]   To our way of thinking, for as far as the eye could see, were Angels and Saints prostrated before the Throne of God, adoring Our Lord and praising and venerating His most holy Mother Mary.   Remember, these men and women had been waiting for the Messiah to come, some for many centuries, or even thousands of years.   It wasn't until Mary's Fiat, her Yes, that the process of their redemption began.   It had always been promised, but it was

---

[4]Luke 1:48-49
[5]Rev 5:11
[6]Rev 14:4-5

not until she said, "*I am the handmaiden of the Lord; let it be done unto me according to His will.*" that it came to pass.

All the paintings we've ever seen of the Coronation, show Mary, breathtakingly beautiful, seated in the center, with Jesus on one side, God the Father on the other, and the Holy Spirit hovering above them. Jesus and the Father hold the crown above the head of our Lady. At that instant, Heaven and earth wait in silent anticipation. When the crown is placed on her head, brilliant lights shoot out to every part of the Heavens, with the message that the Queen has been crowned; her reign begins. Mary is in queenship; we are her subjects. She is our Queen, our Mother, our confidante, our friend. She is the mediatrix between us and our Lord Jesus. She is our voice in Heaven.

How many times have you heard "*I have a problem with the role Mary has in the Church?*" We have no problem with the place our Lord, right from the beginning gave Mother Mary. It was not the Church who called Mary the Mother of God, but Jesus himself. It was Jesus Who set up the pattern we were to follow, that of turning to Mother Mary for help. At Cana, we do not hear of the wedding party going directly to Jesus for help in their dilemma. They could have; He was there, amongst them. No, they must have gone to Mother Mary, or as with us, maybe Mother Mary, the involved Mother noticed her children had problems and she turned to her Son. And how did the Son react to His Mother's request? Although, initially He did not want to handle the problem at that time, it was His Mother's gentle persuasion that moved Jesus' Heart, and He did as she had asked of Him. Was she puffed up because her Son had showed His favor upon her by saying *yes*? No; she turned to the servants and said the words she repeats over and over again, "*Do whatever He tells you.*" Not, "Do whatever I tell you, for I am important." No, in her perfect imitation of her Son Who always deferred to His Father, she humbly deferred to her Son.

Don't turn away from the Lord's Mother. She is there, beside her Son, listening to you, waiting to plead with her Son on your behalf. If you have no problem asking sinners on earth to intercede for you, why hesitate to ask our Blessed Mother who is in Heaven and is *"highly favored by the Lord"* and blessed by all generations?

The events we study in this mystery are most important to us, as children of God. Lucifer had a great deal of trouble consenting to Jesus, God in the second Person, becoming man, and still having to be adored as God. Lucifer knew he had to adore God, but not in the form of a human. After all, he pridefully insisted, the human species were created *far below* the Angels. Worshiping the God-Man Jesus was a tough one to swallow, but the final straw, which pushed him over the edge, was having a *human*, and a *woman* at that, to have dominion over him, to be his Queen. He couldn't handle that. It was this mandate that Lucifer would not accept. He screeched out his battle cry, *"I will not serve!"* And so he was able to incite a band of proud angels and would do battle with God. But one of the lesser Angels rose and with his battle cry: *"Mica-el - Who is like God!"*, he, accompanied by the Angels loyal to God, did battle with Lucifer and the fallen angels. Because they were duped by Lucifer and made the *final* decision for him against God, they broke away from their Creator. And can you imagine how sorrowful God the Father was when 1/3 of the angels left Him.[7] Among Franciscans it is said, that when the angels left, their places (1/3 of all the Angels) in the Kingdom were to be replaced by Franciscans. Since St. Francis lived the true Gospel life, I really believe, the Lord's message of hope

---

[7]And then a second sign appeared in the sky, a huge dragon...Its tail dragged a third of the stars from the sky and dropped them down to the earth. Rev 12:3

is that *all* those who authentically try to live the Gospel will take those empty seats vacated by the fallen angels.[8]

Keep in mind that Lucifer was a *favored* Angel of God. The coronation of Mary had to be an important step in God's eyes, knowing that Lucifer would break away, as a result. Mary has always had a major role in the Kingdom, in the Church. She was given a special title for her *Fiat*. Why? Why should she be given this singular honor? What did she do that was so spectacular? A wise Franciscan priest once told us, "*Mary didn't do anything. She just stood there.*" She emptied herself of all that was Mary, and allowed God to fill her with Jesus. Is there a powerful message here for us, a way to become beloved in the eyes of the Lord? Is Jesus saying to us through Mary, "*Don't just do something; stand there! Empty yourself of all that is not of Me and My Father! I'll do the rest.*"

†

"*Now a great sign appeared in heaven: a woman, adorned with the sun, standing on a moon, and with the twelve stars on her head for a crown.*[9]

†

"*With jewels set in gold...*
"*Dressed in brocades, the King's daughter is led into the King's palace (Heaven) with bridesmaids in her train.*
"*Her ladies-in-waiting follow
and enter the King's Palace to general rejoicing.*
"*Your ancestors will be replaced by sons
whom you will make lords of the whole world.*
"*I shall immortalize your name,
nations will sing your praises forever.*"[10]

---

[8]Rev 12:7-10
[9]Rev 12:1
[10]Psalm 45:13-17

Victories of the Rosary

"All we can do now, is pray!" When all else fails, when there is nothing left to do, we pray. A last ditch effort; we've tried everything else; it's out of our control; now all that is left is to pray. Instead, we should begin by praying, recognizing that the most powerful tool we have is Prayer.

Saint Paul said: *"Put on the armor of God, that you may be able to stand against the wiles of the devil. For our wrestling is not against flesh and blood, but against the Principalities and the Powers, against the world rulers of the present darkness, against the spiritual forces of wickedness on high."*[1]

Now, *we are in the best of times; we are in the worst of times.* Our battle is not with humans, as St. Paul tells us. It is truly a battle, possibly the final battle for our souls and those precious souls of our families. What is the armor of God? What better armor can you wear than that of the Virgin Mary? Who did you run to when you were a child? Wasn't it to Mama? We need our Mama. I remember when I was a child, and I would have a nightmare. Who did I run to? My mother! And what did she say? *"Did you pray before you fell asleep?"* Each time, I had forgotten to pray. Then, when she sent me back to my bed with, *"Now say your prayers and you won't have any more bad dreams."* I really didn't have too much confidence that it would work. Although her reassuring words turned out to be prophecy, I never believed. But, it always worked!

"Put on the armor of God." Who was chosen by God to bring into the world His Son, to care for Him, to parent Him, to teach Him, to protect Him, to love and cherish Him? Was it not Mother Mary? Did Jesus not perform His first Miracle through the intercession of the Blessed Mother? As we

---

[1]Eph 6:11-12

165

journey with Jesus and Mary in this book, we see how many times the Mother of God, and our Mother, interceded for us, how many times she had to make the decision for us, at the cost of her most precious Son.[2] And she said *yes*! If she did that, knowing her Son would suffer, how much more would she do now, as we turn to her, praying the Rosary, the one hundred and fifty roses we place into a bouquet for her.

The Lord and His Mother, the Angels and the Saints have always been interwoven. When we wrote of the Miracles of the Eucharist, we not only learned more about the Holy Eucharist, we discovered Mother Mary and her connection with the Eucharist. We encountered the Saints: how they lived and died for the Eucharist. We learned of the presence of the Angels during the Mass. When we wrote of Mother Mary we became more fervently aware of the Eucharist, the Saints and the Angels. When we wrote of the Saints, we could see the love they had for the Eucharist, how they all turned to Mother Mary and how many relied on the help of the Angels. We could see the work of the Angels in Jesus and Mary's life and in the lives of the Saints.

The greats of our Church turned to the Lord, to His Mother, to the Saints who had come before them, and to the Angels. They knew they needed help and they were not past asking for it. Our Popes all prayed the Rosary. It brought Pope Pius XII through the horrible second World War. Pope John XXIII prayed 15 decades of the Holy Rosary, every day. Our dear Pope John Paul II has a Rosary on him, at all times. In his private chapel, as he prays for guidance and direction from the Lord before the Blessed Sacrament,

---

[2]i.e. When our Lady asked her Son to help at the Wedding Feast of Cana, she had to know that this might possibly be the first step of His ministry, and consequently the first step to the Cross.

When Jesus met His Mother on the way of the Cross, she said nothing; she didn't try to stop Him from going to the Cross. She is called the Co-redemptorist because of her part in our redemption.

you can bet he is turning to the Lady who saved his life May 13th, 1981. Beside his Bible and Office (Breviary) you are sure to find the Rosary. When we interviewed the Archbishop of Zaragoza, and filmed the Shrine of Our Lady of Pilar, we were invited into the Archbishop's private Chapel. As with our beloved Pope John Paul II and Archbishop Fulton Sheen, there beside his Bible, and his Office, was hanging a Rosary!

The Angels and the Rosary

How many times, Dear Friends, have you been there to save us, even from ourselves? Bob and I were still in the business world. On this particular day, I was receiving some very upsetting phone calls from customers and manufacturers. Time came for me to pick up my grandson from high school; he was not old enough to drive. As I drove toward his school, I became concerned that the anger that had invaded my heart and soul might spread to my boy. Seeking peace, as only the Lord and His Mother can provide, I prayed the Rosary for a half hour, right up to the parking lot of his school.

Rob (my grandson) got in the car, and we then tried to get onto the freeway. I was in the far right lane trying to merge into traffic. I could barely squeeze into the slow lane on my left. Cars were barely moving. Finally, having entered it, I tried to get into the faster lanes, to no avail. I was blocked in: first by the car in front, then by the car in the rear, and then by the car on the left who would not move up and give me room to get in, no matter how much I flashed my left-turn signal. Well, this was not helping my former attitude a bit. Now, I was really getting upset!

Suddenly, I felt the car go out of control! I tried to steer the wheel; it was locked! I shot out my right arm to block my grandson from going through the window. I shouted, "No, Lord, not him." The car stopped dead! My foot started to shake. It was still on the brake which had not worked. I had tried to push the brake pedal through the floor board. When my trembling had subsided, I got out of the car on my side. On Rob's side, we were on the edge of a precipice about forty feet above the road below.

A highway patrolman came to our aid. He shook his head and said there was no earthly reason why we were not dead. The tow truck arrived. The driver used some expletives, I will not repeat, and shook his head as he helped us into the cab of his tow truck. Our car was helplessly raised in the air behind us. When we arrived at the gas station, the mechanic dialed the phone for me. I burst into tears, as I tried to tell Bob what had happened. I really didn't know myself.

The mechanic later told Bob if Rob and I were not standing there in front of him, and if the highway policeman had not verified the story, he would not have believed it. He showed us how the axle had snapped in two, severing the wheel from the rest of the car. The wheel should have spun off; we and the car should have capsized and plunged into the road and the cars below. Instead, it became wedged in the fender, and prevented the car from moving and turning over. No one could explain it at the time. They had never seen anything like it. It was as if someone had jammed the wheel, bracing the car.

Was that an Angel who had wedged the wheel beneath the car? Were they Angels who blocked my path, and locked me in the right lane, not allowing us to go into the fast lane? If we had been in the fast lane, we would have been going so fast, not only would we have died but we would have taken other lives with us. There would definitely have been a pile-up. Maybe it was someone else's Angel who interceded. Maybe it was the Guardian Angel of someone who would discover the cure for Cancer.

Or could it be, it was that God heard my cry and called upon our Guardian Angels to save my grandson? Or was it the Queen of Angels to whom I had been praying the Rosary before I picked up my grandson. Had She summoned her army of

Angels? After all, our grandson had always loved her. He had been in the Junior Legion of Mary when he was a little boy. Did she have a special plan for him?[3]

†

We believe that all wars are Religious Wars, all battles between Principalities and Powers, good fighting evil. We fight with guns and bombs instead of prayer. Mothers' sons and daughters die; families lose their husbands and fathers, wives and mothers, sisters and brothers; and the world is poorer for the loss of these precious loved ones. But it doesn't have to be that way. We have a more powerful form of combat - on our knees. These are just a few instances where Mother Mary was asked for her intervention through the Rosary, and she said *yes!*

I know that there are countless more examples of battles fought and won through the Rosary, but forgive us if we just cite these few.

The Battle of Lepanto - 1571

It was the sixteenth century, and the Body of Christ was being attacked from all sides. On one side, poor innocent believers were falling to an enemy from within the Church. The Church in Europe would lose 6,000,000 of her most precious, faithful children to heresy. As they did not know what was happening, they did not fight. They did not pray for our Mother Mary's intervention. And so, they were lost to us. Praise God, they are now coming back home to their Church, and they are so very beautiful. Could it be the many rosaries said by their families and friends?

As this sneak attack was going on, other enemies of the Church were attacking. Turkish forces were overtaking much of Christian Europe. As this wave of followers of Mohammed invaded a country, they not only took lives, they

---

[3]from the book: *"Heavenly Army of Angels"* by Bob and Penny Lord

took souls. The name of Christ was not heard in these lands for up to 700 years. They knew that they would never be able to subjugate their conquests unless they could take away all hope. Had Satan told them of his motto over the gates of hell, "*All you who enter here, abandon all hope.*"

But they were not victorious where people prayed! The Turkish fleet was attacking Austria. The Austrian fleet under Don Juan was no match against the superior Turkish fleet. It looked as if another country would be lost to Islam. Her family is in danger? They need her? Mary to the rescue! Pope Pius V sent out word to the forces of Christ, to pray the Rosary. A Rosary Crusade was waged on the knees of the faithful, and the battle was won.

To the eyes of the world, the Austrian fleet was outnumbered. But there was a powerful general that could not be seen by human eyes. It was Mary and her Heavenly Army of Angels! Although the Austrian fleet appeared finished, they were not. They were joined by the Angels, with Michael the Archangel in front. Swords of faith drawn, they were poised, just waiting for their Queen's command. The Image of Our Lady of Guadalupe was placed at the helm of the ship leading the Austrian fleet into battle, to victory.

Man's weapons could not defend their land, but roses in the form of rosary beads moved Jesus' Heart and through His Mother Mary, He did the rest. *Jesus, I trust in You*!

Vienna - 1683

We're in the seventeenth century and the Turkish forces are still forging ahead, hell-bent on conquering and subjugating all of Christian Europe. We find ourselves in Vienna, in 1683. The Emperor of Austria's forces are exhausted and discouraged. They are badly outnumbered and weary from battle. The Emperor in a last ditch effort, sends word to King John Sobieski, Sovereign of Poland, imploring his help.

Now, this was not the first time that King Sobieski faced overwhelming odds in battle. But the pendulum swung so overpoweringly in the enemy's favor, he did not know if this was to be his death rather than his victory. As the Turkish invaders were converging on Vienna, King John Sobieski turned to Our Lady of Czestochowa: *"Give us victory, My Lady, grant us your help and salvation. As for me, do whatever you choose. I'll accept your will, whether it's life or death."*

Suddenly a thought came to him: "Instead of honoring her (Mother Mary), we have passed a lot of responsibility on to her. Seeking honor and glory for ourselves, we've left the toil to her. But she has accepted it. I don't know why she loves us, yet she does love us, even if we repay her with ingratitude and disloyalty."

"Give us victory," he prayed, *"and let it be your victory alone."* He came before the people and asked them to join him in publicly placing all their trust in Our Lady. He knelt humbly before his Queen, Mary most holy and one by one all the people knelt with him. He began the Apostles Creed, reminding them what they believed, and what so many before them had died for. All the faithful prayed, only now, the prayers took on different meaning. They were no longer just words; they were a battle hymn: This is what we believe; and for this we die, rather than deny our Lord.

As they continued the Rosary, now reciting the Lord's prayer, the words *"thy Will be done"* took on new meaning. They were truly commending their lives to the Father, self-abandonment, the trust of children, of whom Jesus said: *"The Kingdom of Heaven is theirs"*. The King placed his troops and all of Vienna under the protection of Our Blessed Mother. Man, woman and child, peasant and noble, King and soldier all intoned, with one voice and one hope, the supplication, "*Mary help us*". And help them, she did.

80,000 Christian troops, with King John Sobieski in front, defeated a fierce Turkish army consisting of 250,000 barbarians.

Now, the Turkish army was known for their inhumane treatment of soldiers and citizens. The mere thought of them approaching a village would bring terror into the hearts of men as well as women. What gave these people the courage to fight and win? The Mother of God, "*Mary, Help of all Christians*". What gave them the power and the ammunition to use against the enemy? The Rosary!

Sri Lanka (Ceylon) - 1940's

World War II was raging and ravaging nation after nation in Europe and in Asia. No country was safe from the relentless forging ahead, onslaught of the godless Nazi and merciless Japanese forces. World War I, "*the war to end all wars*" had done no such thing. Adolf Hitler, the man everyone thought was a harmless maniac, no one to pay any attention to, was conquering most of Western Europe. The tiny nation of Japan, which was negotiating with our government right up to the sneak attack on Pearl Harbor, was determined to rule the rest of the world.

The atrocities that our service men shared after they returned home gave us a clue to the inhumane torture they underwent in prison camps. The rules governing the treatment of prisoners, that had been set up by the Geneva Convention, before World War I, did not seem to apply to the members of the Axis, as the Nazi-Japanese alliance was called. They acted as if they were exempt from this governing body which was given the authority to insure humanitarian treatment to all prisoners of war. The Nurenburg trials brought out the open defiance of the Nazis as witnesses came forth, testifying to the monstrous genocide and barbaric experimentation done on civilians as well as prisoners of war.

The Japanese fleet was ominously approaching the tiny nation of Sri Lanka. They were not equipped, in the smallest way, to defend themselves against the powerful Japanese Navy. It seemed all was lost. Then, the Bishop of Sri Lanka turned to Mother Mary. He knew that her Son Jesus would not refuse her anything. He promised the Lord he would build a Cathedral in His Mother's honor if they were saved from the enemy that was almost upon them. He placed his small island under the protection of Mother Mary. We can just see Mother Mary covering them with her mantle, blocking the people of Sri lanka as they knelt praying the Rosary. We can see her *Heavenly Army of Angels* spreading their wings, swords drawn. Did they blind the eyes of the invading fleet so that they could not see the small nation? *No one knows!* But as resolutely as they had been converging on Sri Lanka, they turned around and did not attack the small island. Why had they left them alone? Ask Jesus and Mary when you see them!

Austria - 1950's

Many of the Catholics in Germany, who refused to follow Hitler and his henchmen, suffered at the hands of the S.S. and the Gestapo. Thousands were sent to Concentration Camps. In one village, where there is a Shrine to Our Lady of Alt Otting, near Munich, on the eve of the end of the war, a Priest and six villagers were executed. What was their crime? They had gone to the Allied forces to plead with them to not harm the Shrine to Our Lady. For this, the Nazis brutally murdered them.

The shadow of the hammer and sickle was covering more and more of Eastern Europe. As Hitler scorched the earth, the Soviet troops watched and waited. They would have their fun, next. In 1945, the Second World War ended, but for too many that did not mean peace. Instead a new enemy was marching. God alone knew what horrors that would mean. The people of Austria waited and trembled.

Their worst fears came to pass. Russian troops occupied their land. A feeling of helplessness began to spread through the villages; the faithful began to turn to the Mother of God, their Maria. They could not fight with man's weapons; they were plainly outnumbered. They would fight on their knees. They prayed as if with one mind and heart, families, whole villages, men and women alike, the young and the old, the rich and the poor, all pleading for Our Lady's intervention.

They had been forced to hail Hitler (Heil Hitler). And many of their families had died rather than pay tribute to this pagan who had set himself up as God. Now, as they prayed the Fifteen decades of the Holy Rosary, they hailed their Mother and their Lord Jesus. And their Heavenly Family heard them and came through. The Russian troops just turned around and marched out of Austria. Without any *worldly* reasoning, the Russian troops just pulled out. There was no explanation ever given why they just upped and left. As quickly as they had appeared, they disappeared.

What made them do it? Could it be that the Mother of God, their Maria, and her Son, summoned Their Heavenly Army of Angels and with the Rosary as ammunition, the Russians, knowing they were outnumbered, retreated?

Brazil - 1960's

Brazil has always been a country of the haves and the have nots. The poor get poorer and the rich get richer. The many poor live in cardboard houses, while the few rich live in mansions. Sanitary conditions are virtually unknown for most of the citizens of Brazil. It is a nation of many Old Testament Lazarus' who would relish some scraps from the tables of their own "*rich man*".

It is a natural breeding ground for Communism to infiltrate and spread. When your child's stomach is swollen from starvation and his lips are parched from lack of water, when you see your family dying before your eyes because their is no medical aid for them, any promise of hope sounds better than what you have.

It looked as if an even greater monster would swallow up the innocent souls of Brazil. It was the eve of the elections. The Communist party had campaigned well and hard. It was a shoo-in. Victory was certain! The celebrations had already begun in the Communist Party Headquarters. Did the poor not realize they were, like so many of their Hispanic brothers and sisters, only trading one kind of inequity for another?

Who would tell them? There was no other voice they would listen to. The Communists made it sound so good. They had promised them change. And any change was better than what they had. The poor would have a chance at education, health care, better living conditions, benefits from Big Brother (the Communist Party) unlike anything they had ever dreamed of. It sounded so good! It looked as if the faithful, the poor who had no earthly wealth, only Heavenly riches, would trade in their God and their Mother Mary for the godless paganism of Communism, without even knowing that was what they were doing.

Dusk had fallen. The streets were dark, except for some lights streaming out from the buildings. Suddenly, light started to cut through the darkness. It seemed far off, almost diffused, flickering. From a distance, it appeared as if waves of rays were flowing upward toward Heaven. As the light came closer, all the eye could see were Brazilian women processing, carrying candles, singing litanies to our Lady and praying the Rosary. They, like so many of us, when we are in danger, were crying out to Mama. And she was turning to her Son, as she did at Cana. And He was now, not changing water into wine; He was changing men' hearts of stone into hearts made for Him alone. Through the Rosary, it was as if Jesus was walking the earth once more, and the veils were lifting from the people's eyes, and they could see the Communists for who they were.

The *sure* Victory became the *surprising*, but *devastating* Defeat!

The Philippines - 1980's

The citizens of the Philippines had suffered at the hands of President Marcos and his wife Imelda, who made a sport out of selfish, excessive spending while their people starved. How the people had loved President Marcos! How they had embraced him and his bride. How they in turn had betrayed them. It seemed as if there was no hope for the people. When someone attempted to better conditions and try by election to bring about reform, he was killed. Cory Aquino's husband was such a man. He was returning to Manila to run for office against President Marcos. He was assassinated as he deplaned the aircraft, in front of his wife and family.

Cory Aquino fearlessly rose up to continue her husband's mission. And, the people responded. They went out into the streets and processed, walls of humanity marching forward, flowers in one hand and rosaries in the other, fingering the beads of their rosaries as tanks with their young men came toward them. When it seemed as if neither side would give in, suddenly the soldiers climbed down from their tanks and joined the faithful, taking beads into their hand, their guns replaced by the armor of God, the Rosary.

There are those who say, Our Lady appeared in the sky, to the soldiers in Marcos' army, and pleaded with them not to hurt her children. There is a statue there in the square, to commemorate this time when despair disappeared and hope appeared, when for a moment the world could see the day when the *"lion would lay down with the lamb"*!

Is there power in the Rosary? The Rosary has lived on, in the hands of the faithful, in freedom and in captivity. But in a few years, a man and a woman, who had the power to do good but chose evil, will be forgotten.

As we have been writing about the Victories of the Rosary, we started to understand what we believe the Lord is saying through this book: There is hope! Be not afraid! See how I have responded when you have turned to My Mother through the Rosary. I have given you a means, a gift. All you have to do is reach out and pray. I am listening!

Our Lady of Prompt Succor comes to Louisiana

The city of New Orleans in the Louisiana territory was originally a French settlement in 1718, then became a Spanish settlement in 1763, and then again a French settlement, before Napoleon Bonaparte sold it to the United States in 1803. This can all be said in one sentence, but the ramifications of such change were monumental.

A little community of French Ursuline nuns came to New Orleans in 1727, to educate the settlers, and help in the hospital. All went well until 1763 when the city came under Spanish rule. Many Spaniards came, and with them Spanish nuns. Now the Ursulines were predominantly Spanish, with a remnant of French nuns.

In 1800, the French took back New Orleans. It was only eleven years since the French Revolution had devastated France, and most particularly, the *religious* in France. Tales reached the Mother Superior of the Ursulines (who was Spanish), of whole communities of nuns being decapitated, subjected to inhumane atrocities, priests exiled or killed in France. She feared for her community. She wrote to the King of Spain, Charles IV, asking permission to leave New Orleans immediately with her sisters. Soon after having sent the petition, she and fifteen Spanish nuns left for Havana.

All that was left were seven French Ursulines, but they kept everything going. The Mother Superior, Mother St. André Madier, longed for the strength of her cousin, Mother St. Michel. She wrote, pleading with Mother St. Michel to come to New Orleans and take charge of the community. She was well known for her leadership ability and piety. Mother St. Michel was strong, having gone underground when the Revolution began. In the south of France, with the help of another woman, she had begun to rebuild her community, and open a girls' boarding school in Montpelier. When she received word from Mother André, of their plight she dropped everything and set out for the New World.

That's when the trouble began, and Our Lady was put in charge. Mother St. Michel appealed first to her Spiritual Director. He refused her permission to leave France. The state of the religious communities in France was a shambles. A woman of her qualifications was needed in France. He sent her to the Bishop. His refusal was even louder than the Spiritual Director. He almost screamed at her, *"The Pope alone can give this authorization....the Pope alone!"*

Now if you consider that Pope Pius VII was imprisoned by Napoleon, and being transported from Rome to Versailles, and that he was completely incommunicado, you can realize the futility of the whole situation. However, Mother St. Michel was a feisty nun. She wrote a letter to the Pope anyway. The thrust of her letter was as follows:

"Most Holy Father, I appeal to your Apostolic tribunal. I am ready to submit to your decision. Speak. Faith teaches me that you are the voice of the Lord. I await your orders. "Go" or "Stay" from Your Holiness, will be the same to me."

The letter had been written for three months, but there had been no way to post it. The conditions of the country were such that nothing was secure. So Mother Superior addressed Our Lady: *"O Most Holy Virgin Mary, if you obtain a prompt and favorable answer to my letter, I promise to have you honored in New Orleans under the title of* **Our Lady of Prompt Succor**[4]*."* Part of the deal with our Lady was that a statue would be carved, which would be brought to New Orleans and made the protectress of the community.

Nobody acts more quickly than Mother Mary when she wants something done. Mother St. Michel's letter left Montpelier on March 19, 1809, and permission was granted by His Holiness April 28. She left for Louisiana with her statue of Our Lady. She kept her word to Our Lady. As soon as she and her little group of nuns arrived in New Orleans, Our Lady's statue was placed in the Convent Chapel, under the title of *Our Lady of Prompt Succor.*

Devotion spread throughout New Orleans, even into other areas of Louisiana. There are two memorable miracles attributed to Our Lady of Prompt Succor's intervention:

The first is the great fire of 1812.

The entire city of New Orleans was being ravaged by a devastating fire, which was fanned by incredible winds. The fire was heading straight for the little convent. One of the sisters place a statue of Our Lady of Prompt Succor in the window, and prayed for the aid of Mother Mary under this title. Within minutes, the winds made a forty-five degree turn in the other direction. Witnesses who saw the miracle[5] proclaimed: *"Our Lady of Prompt Succor has saved us!".*

---

[4]Prompt Succor means Prompt Help. It is of French derivation.

[5]We had a similar miracle in California, through the intercession of a statue of Our Lady of Fatima, which we had brought back from Fatima, Portugal. An infamous California brushfire was raging on the hill in back of our house. We were ordered to evacuate as the fire was upon us. We knelt before the statue of Our Lady of Fatima, in front of a huge picture window, and as we were praying, we could see the fire make a right angle and turn away from our home, as if running down the hill.

The Battle of New Orleans in 1815

One of the most famous incidents of Our Lady of Prompt Succor's intervention in the city of New Orleans was during the Battle of New Orleans in 1815. Andrew Jackson's troops were greatly outnumbered by the British, their naval power far greater than anything we could handle. It was time for Mary. Mothers, wives, daughters, and sisters of the men fighting the great battle, flocked to the little Ursuline Chapel on the evening of January 7, 1815, and prayed the entire night. In the morning, these faithful servants of Mary, not having had any sleep, joined in the Sacrifice of the Mass, celebrated by a future Bishop of New Orleans, Fr. William Dubourg. At Communion time, a carrier brought news: *The British had been defeated; the city of New Orleans had been saved.* Once more, Our Lady of Prompt Succor had come to the rescue of her people.

The statue of Our Lady of Prompt Succor remains in the little Ursuline Chapel in New Orleans, which has since been renamed the National Shrine to Our Lady of Prompt Succor. A yearly Mass of Thanksgiving is sung on January 8 of each year. The Shrine has been given esteemed honors from the Holy See. On September 27, 1851, Pope Pius IX authorized the celebration of the Feast of Our Lady of Prompt Succor, and the singing of the Mass on January 8 each year. In 1894, Pope Leo XIII issued a decree, granting the "*Solemn Coronation of the Miraculous Statue of Our Lady of Prompt Succor, exposed to public veneration in the Chapel of the Ursuline Convent, New Orleans*".

The Shrine to Our Lady of Prompt Succor is a powerful, authentic American Shrine in honor of the Mother of God, and in thanksgiving for all the favors granted through her intercession. Mary said to us at the Rue du Bac in Paris, when she gave us the Miraculous Medal in 1830, "**But come to the foot of the altar; great graces will be poured out to those who ask for them.**" Many tourists come to New

Orleans every year for any number of reasons, including Mardi Gras. Take time to visit this powerful Shrine of Our Lady right here in our own country. Come to the foot of the Altar. She is waiting here for you. The address is

National Shrine of Our Lady of Prompt Succor
2635 State Street - New Orleans, LA 70118

Particular thanks and credit must be given to Dr. Paul Hatrel, of New Orleans, whom we met on our first visit to New Orleans in 1987, and who gave us this information.

New Orleans 1990

We see on our supposedly non-biased news reports on television, scenes of violence (often orchestrated by media cameramen) which show men and women, who are trying to defend defenseless unborn babies from being murdered, in an unsympathetic light. We do not approve of violence in any form, but we do take issue with the fuss made because of damage to buildings and the total disregard of the murdering of innocent unborn American children.

Why do we not see in the newspapers, and hear on television, about the faithful who fight on their knees with the Rosary as their sword? In New Orleans, a group of Pro-Lifers prayed 15 decades of the Holy Rosary outside of an abortion clinic (Delta Women's Clinic). Members of the *Rosary Novena for Life* had been processing for months prior to this day. The Clinic was closed down within a week...on Magnificat's Day of the Rosary Congress.[6]

✝

Our Lady of the Holy Rosary, in this time of need for our Church and our country, please accept our prayers and ask your Son for mercy on us and our families.

---

[6]We thank Father Harold F. Cohen, S.J., in particular, for his invaluable help in our presenting many of the victories of the Rosary in this chapter.

The History of the Rosary

As we stand in awe before the majestic Basilica of the Rosary at Lourdes, who is there (above the entrance) to welcome us inside, but Our Lady handing St. Dominic the Rosary in 1208. No matter what we write about, the message that seems to resound over and over again is: "*In times of Crisis, the Lord gives us Saints and Other Powerful Men and Women in our Church, Miracles of the Eucharist, Apparitions by Our Lady, intercession of the Angels, and powerful weapons to get us through the Pilgrimage of life.*" The Rosary is one of those weapons and nowhere has there been a time when that statement was truer, or the Rosary more needed.

By 1208, the heresy of Albigensianism which had started in Southern France, in the Eleventh Century, had become a deadly cancer threatening the entire Church.[1]

St. Dominic

The Church is in danger, God raises up a Saint! The Lord gave St. Dominic the mandate to fight Albigensianism, and bring back those who had left the Church. He fought with all he was worth to defeat this heresy, but it was an uphill fight all the way. He prayed for help. The Angels brought his prayer to the feet of Our Lady. Now, Our Lady loved Dominic dearly; he was one of her Son's special priests and friends. How could she not help him? One night in 1208, while St. Dominic was hard at prayer in the Chapel of Notre Dame de la Prouille, Our Lady appeared to him. She was holding the Rosary. She said to him,

"*Be of good courage, Dominic; the fruits of your labor shall be abundant. The remedy for the evils which you lament will be meditation on the life, death and glory of my Son, uniting thereto the recitation of the Angelic*

---

[1]This is just one of the heresies Bob and Penny wrote about, in detail, in their book: "*Scandal of the Cross and Its Triumph*".

Salutation (Hail Mary) by which the mystery of redemption was announced to the world.

"This devotion you are to inculcate by your preaching, is a practice most dear to my Son and to me - as a most powerful means of dissipating heresy, extinguishing vice, propagating virtue, imploring divine mercy, and obtaining my protection. I desire that not only you, but all those who shall enter your Order, perpetually promote this manner of prayer. The faithful will obtain by it innumerable advantages and will always find me ready to aid them in their wants. This is the precious gift which I leave to you and to your spiritual children."

St. Dominic and his followers preached on the values of the Rosary, and the Albigensianism heresy was defeated. He gave credit to the intercession of *Our Lady of the Rosary*.

Simon de Montfort attributed his victory over the Albigensians, in the critical battle of Muret, to the intercession of Our Lady and the Rosary. In thanksgiving, he built the first Rosary Chapel in Muret.

Blessed Alan de Roche

When the crisis was over, the people forgot their need for Our Lady's help, and the Rosary went on the back burner. While it had become a strong part of the Dominican spirituality, and most of the Religious Orders prayed some form of the Rosary, the rank and file by and large, abandoned the devotion. It took another Dominican, Alan de Roche of France, in the Fifteenth Century to put the Rosary on a solid footing.

De Roche had a great love for Our Lady. He took every opportunity to spread devotion to the Lady's Rosary. Prior to his time, there had been many variations on the Rosary. Some prayed the five sorrows, others the seven sorrows. Some prayed fifteen decades, using scripture passages. Alan de Roche formalized the Rosary into the fifteen decades we pray today, using the format we use, beginning with the Creed, then the Our Father and ten Hail Mary's, followed by the Glory Be. He traveled through Germany, where the people were not familiar with the devotion to the Rosary. He was able to get devotion accepted so well, he began a **Confraternity of the Rosary**.

It began in the Cathedral of Cologne. It was 1470. The Germans were going through a terrible war. The faithful gathered around the central altar in the Cathedral at Cologne, and prayed the Rosary for peace. When peace came, through impossible odds, credit was given to the intercession of Our Lady. As soon as the war ended, De Roche used the triumph to press home to the rulers of the country, the role Our Lady of the Rosary played in their victory. He suggested a feast of Thanksgiving. He also asked the emperor to arrange with the Pope for an international Confraternity of the Rosary to be established. The emperor was the first to affix his name to the register of the Confraternity, and you can be assured he was followed by all the people in the kingdom.

The results were miraculous. Within a few months, there were five thousand members of the Confraternity. By the end of the year, over fifty thousand had signed their support for this beautiful gift of Our Lady. The message spread, and within 25 years, there were confraternities all over the world.

St. Louis Marie de Montfort

Moving to the Eighteenth Century, we come to perhaps the most popular prophet of the Rosary, St. Louis Marie de Montfort, who has been given the title, "*Apostle of the Cross and the Holy Rosary*". He spent his entire priesthood espousing the virtues and benefits of the Rosary, as well as the *True Devotion to Mary*, and *Consecration to Mary*. In this century, more Catholics follow the teachings of St. Louis

Marie de Montfort than any other source, with regards to Our Lady. When we were videotaping in Poland, we discovered that our Pope John Paul II, when he was working in the factory, would read Louis Marie de Montfort's book, *True Devotion to Mary* during his lunch time, and again in the evening, committing it to memory.

St. Louis Marie de Montfort wrote in **The Secret of the Holy Rosary**:

"From the time Saint Dominic established the devotion to the holy Rosary up to the time when Blessed Alan de la Roche re-established it, it has always been called the Psalter (Psalms) of Jesus and Mary. This is because it has the same number of Hail Marys as there are psalms in the Book of the Psalms of David (150). Since simple and uneducated people are not able to say the Psalms of David, the Rosary is held to be just as fruitful for them as David's Psalter is for others.

"But the Rosary can be considered to be even more valuable than the latter for three reasons:

†

"1. Firstly, because the Angelic Psalter bears a nobler fruit, that of the Word Incarnate, whereas David's Psalter only prophesies His coming;

†

"2. Just as the real thing is more important than its prefiguration and the body surpasses the shadow, so the Psalter of our Lady is greater than David's Psalter, which did no more than pre-figure it;

†

"3. Because Our Lady's Psalter or the Rosary made up of the Our Father and Hail Mary is the direct work of the Blessed Trinity."

†

In addition, St. Louis says *"They* (the ordinary people) *considered, which is indeed true, that the Heavenly praises of the Rosary contained all the Divine Secrets of the psalms, for, if* the psalms sing of the One who is to come, the Rosary proclaims Him as having come.

"*That is how they began to call their prayer of 150 Salutations 'The Psalter of Mary' and to precede each decade with an Our Father, as was done by those who recited the psalms.*"[2]

†

Our Popes all had a devotion to the Holy Rosary:

On September 17, 1569, **Pope St. Pius V** promulgated devotion to the Rosary, and because of the Christians' victory in Lepanto over the Muslims, he inaugurated an annual commemoration to *Our Lady of the Victory.* Speaking of the Rosary, he wrote:

"*It is the Psalter of Mary, in which the Blessed Mother of God is greeted 150 times with the Angelical salutation (Hail Mary), corresponding to the Psalms of the Psalter of David, together with one Our Father for every ten Hail Marys, and also certain mediations that present the entire life of Jesus Christ.*"[3]

When the Muslims were once again defeated, on the feast of Our Lady of the Snow, August 5, 1716, **Pope Clement XI** attributed the victory to the Rosary.   In gratitude to Our Lady, he placed the Feast of the holy Rosary on the Universal Calendar.

The First Council of Baltimore in 1846 proclaimed Our Mother Mary: "*Mary in her Immaculate Conception Principal Patron of the United States.*"

The Bishops of the United States on February 7, 1847 affirmed it by: "*...unanimously placing the Catholic Church under the special patronage of the Blessed Virgin.*"

Pope Leo XIII declared on October 2, 1898: "*The true form of the Rosary is to be preserved, in reference to the beads by making them up into five, ten, or fifteen decades: likewise*

---

[2]Secrets of the Holy Rosary, # 22

[3]The name "Our Lady's Psalter" can be traced back to the 13th century.

that other beads, of whatever form, are not to be known by the name of Rosary.[4]

Pope Pius XII on October 31, 1942, consecrated the world to the Immaculate Heart of Mary. On November 1, 1950, on the *"Holy Year"*, he declared the Dogma of the Assumption of the Blessed Virgin into Heaven.

We truly believe she was preparing us that far back to do battle with the enemies of the Church through the Mysteries of the Rosary.

Pope Pius XII in his Encyclical Letter on the Rosary, September 15, 1951, declares: *"It is above all, in the bosom of the family that we desire the custom of the Holy Rosary to be everywhere adopted, religiously preserved and ever more intensely practiced. While running your fingers over the beads of the Rosary, do not forget those who languish miserably in prison camps, jails and concentration camps.*

"We do not hesitate to affirm again publicly that we put great confidence in the Holy Rosary for the healing of the evils which afflict our times."

On October 11, 1954, **Pope Pius XII** proclaimed the universal *Feast of the Queenship of Mary*, to be celebrated every year in the whole world on May 31.

Sadly, space and time will not allow us to tell you of the devotion and reliance on the power of the Holy Rosary that our Popes have had over the centuries, up till today!

†

We have just returned from Poland and Rome. We had the privilege of staying in Pope John Paul's Polish Pilgrim House and Cultural Center in Rome. All the paintings and mementos were evidence of the Cross and the Resurrection. But one thing that stands out in my heart at this moment is

---

[4]Be cautious! There are New Age cults that are using the title *"Rosary"* to ensnare you; but what they have done is changed the words and are against God. Check on all books that appear to be for Mary or of the Church with someone who is faithful to the Magisterium.

the Rosary that a priest made out of bread and water, secretly molding what little bread and water ration he had (in the concentration camp), to form a bouquet of roses to his Mother, Mary Most Holy. And she brought him through his (so like that of her Son's) aloneness in his cell, without nourishment and life of any kind beside him to comfort him.

†††

The 15 promises Our Lady gave to us through St. Dominic and then his successor, Blessed Alan de Roche.

†

1.   To those who recite my Rosary devoutly, I promise my special protection.

†

2.   To those who perseveringly say the Rosary, I will reserve some very special grace.

†

3.   The Rosary shall be like strong armor against Hell; it will destroy vice and rout heresy.

†

4.   The Rosary shall make virtue and good triumph; it shall substitute in hearts a love of God for love of the world and raise men's hearts to seek Heaven.

†

5.   Those who entrust themselves to me through the Rosary shall not perish.

†

6.   Those who recite my Rosary with piety, meditating on the mysteries, shall not be overwhelmed with misfortune; neither shall they die a bad death.

†

7.   Those truly devoted to my Rosary shall not die without the consolations of the Church.

†

8.　Those who recite my Rosary shall find during their life and at the moment of death the light of God, the fullness of His grace and they will share in the merits of the blessed.

†

9.　I will promptly deliver from Purgatory those souls who were devoted to my Rosary.

†

10.　The true children of my Rosary shall enjoy great glory in Heaven.

†

11.　What you ask through my Rosary, you shall obtain.

†

12.　Those who spread devotion to my Rosary shall receive from me aid in all their needs.

†

13.　I have obtained from my Son the assurance that devotees of my Rosary shall have as their friends in life and in death the Saints of Heaven.

†

14.　Those who recite my Rosary faithfully are my children - truly the brothers and sisters of my Son, Jesus Christ.

†

15.　Devotion to my Rosary is a special sign of predilection.[5]

†

The History of the Rosary is not over by any means. There are lovers of Our lady, who will bring the Rosary into the Twenty-First Century. Because one thing we know, from our research of the Rosary, it will reign until the end of time. And for those of us who believe in the power Our Lord Jesus has given us through Our Mother Mary, the spread of this devotion will become greater, and greater than ever before in the history of the world, and of the Church.

---

[5]Being specially called

Journeys of Faith

1-800-633-2484   1-504-863-2546

Books

Bob and Penny Lord are authors of best sellers:
This Is My Body, This Is My Blood;
Miracles of the Eucharist
$8.95 Paperback only

The Many Faces Of Mary, A Love Story
$8.95 Paperback $12.95 Hardcover

We Came Back To Jesus
$8.95 Paperback $12.95 Hardcover

Saints and Other Powerful Women in the Church
$12.95 Paperback only

Saints and Other Powerful Men in the Church
$14.95 Paperback only

Heavenly Army of Angels
$12.95 Paperback only

Scandal of the Cross and Its Triumph
$12.95 Paperback only

The Rosary - The Life of Jesus and Mary
$12.95 Hardcover only

Martyrs - They died for Christ
$12.95 Paperback only

Please add $3.00 S&H for first book: $1.00 each add'l book - Louisiana. Res. add 8.25% Tax

Videos and On-site Documentaries

Bob and Penny Lord's Video Series based on their books:
Miracles of the Eucharist - 5 part series filmed at EWTN
Eucharistic Retreat series - 9 part - Bob and Penny & Father Harold Cohen
Saints and Other Powerful Women in the Church
10 part series filmed at EWTN with on-site footage.
Saints and Other Powerful Men in the Church
12 part series filmed at EWTN with on-site footage

Documentaries filmed on-site at the Shrines

The Many Faces of Mary - 16 part series
Many other on-site Documentaries based on
Miracles of the Eucharist,
Mother Mary's Apparitions,
Saints and other Powerful Men and Women in the Church,
and the Heavenly Army of Angels.
New Audio Series - Request our list of videos and audios.

Pilgrimages

Journey in Faith on a Pilgrimage with Bob and Penny Lord and their ministry to the Shrines of Europe, the Holy Land, and the Shrines of Mexico every year.

Learn more about your Faith. Celebrate Holy Mass each day at the Shrines. Every Pilgrimage is a Renewal of Faith, and a Retreat.

Come and join them on one of these special Pilgrimages. Call for more information, and ask for our latest pilgrimage brochure.

Lecture Series

Bob and Penny travel to all parts of the world to spread the Good News.
They speak on what they have written about in their books;
the Body of Christ, through the Miracles of the Eucharist, the Mother of Christ, through her Apparitions,
the Men and Women Saints and how the Lord has worked in their lives, using their yes! to save His Church,
the Angels, and the place they have had in the life of Jesus and Mary and the Church,
the Martyrs, and the message the Lord is sending to the people of God.

Conferences

Bob and Penny have spoken at Conferences in the United States, Mexico and Europe.

They feel called to meet and share with the faithful of the Roman Catholic Church the treasure we have:
Our Lord in His Holy Eucharist,
Our Mother Mary and her part in our lives,
our brothers and sisters the Saints, our role models
in this world of false heroes,
and the Angels whom the Lord has given to us
to protect and guide us.

Good Newsletter

We are publishers of the Good Newsletter, which is printed four times a year.
This Newsletter provides timely articles,
on our Faith,
on the Eucharist,
Mother Mary,
the Saints, Angels, Martyrs,
current events affecting our Church,
and consequently we, the People of God.
It also keeps you informed of the activities of our community.

Bibliography

Butler, Thurston, Atwater - *Lives of the Saints*
    Christian Classics - Westminster, Md 1980

Dictionary of Mary - Catholic Book Publishing Co. 1985

Fernandez, Francis - *In Conversation with God*
    Scepter Press Inc. - New Rochelle NY 1989

De Montfort, Louis St. - *God Alone*
    Montfort Publications Bay Shore NY 1987

McKenzie John L S.J - *Dictionary of the Bible*
    Mac Millan Publishing NY 1985

O'Carroll Michael Fr. CS Sp - *Theotokos*
    Michael Glazier Inc. - Wilmington, DE 1982

Sheridan, John V. Msgr. - *We Pray for World Peace*
    The Rosary Hour Inc. - Los Angeles, CA

Sr. Mary Agreda - *The City of God 4 vols.*
    Ave Maria Institute - Washington NJ 1971